Active English DISCUSSION

Andrew Finch

1

> *This book is dedicated to Heebon, without whom it could not have been written. Thank you for all the wonderful hints and suggestion, and for all your contributions, especially just being there. you have helped to make this book what it is.*
>
> *Thank you.*

Preface

When we discuss, we use thinking skills such as problem-solving, critical thinking, deduction, inference, reasoning and summarizing. We also express our ideas and opinions simply and clearly, using persuasion, suggestion, agreement and negotiation. *Active English Discussion 1* helps students develop these skills in English, in a cooperative learning environment that focuses on group-work, creativity and mutual respect. Each Unit develops the vocabulary, phrases and techniques needed for discussion and debate, helping students share the ideas, beliefs and values that are important to them.

In order to do this, the eight pages in each Unit follow a similar structure, building the language, ideas and discussion skills step by step. This gradual, student centered approach promotes the informed sharing of facts and opinions that is the essence of true discussion:

Page 1: Pre-reading. Studentsactivate the "reading schema," exploring the topic together before reading, discussing, debating, or making role-playsabout it. These activities are mostly interactive, preparing students for group-work.

Page 2: Topic-reading. This section presents a reading passage about the topic of the Unit, introducing key vocabulary and concepts. Students can listen to this passage on the CD-Rom accompanying the book. Further follow-up reading passages are offered on the Pearson website.
- **Match the Words:** Key words from the passage are presented in a matching format, encouraging students to extend or confirm their store of vocabulary.

Page 3: While-reading: Comprehension and Extension.Students check and expand their knowledge and understanding.
- **Comprehension Check:** These questions help students to review the reading passage in greater detail.
- **Think for Yourself:** These questions invite students to creatively explore the issues in the reading passage.
- **Background Information:** Further information useful for discussion and debate is offered here. This can motivate students to find more facts and figures by themselves.

Page 4: Post-reading: Discussion. Students have sufficient vocabulary and information by now to express their opinions on questions related to the topic of the Unit. However, a useful sub-section isaddedat the bottom of the page:
- **Conversation Strategies:** These gambits offer helpful idioms and phrases to be used in the discussion.

Page 5: Role-Play: Dialogue. Students listen to the dialogue on the CD-Rom and then take on the roles of the characters, exploring the main topic in a conversational, informal manner, before making their own role-plays.

- **Key Words and Expressions:** Idioms and expressions from the dialogue are highlighted and explained.
- **Dialogue Quiz:** These quizzes invite students to discover more about the ideas in the dialogue.

Page 6: Getting Ready. In preparation for the role-plays or debates which appear on page 7 of each Unit, students think of ideas for their role or their side of the debate, using various methods, including brainstorming and outlining. Appropriate phrases and idioms are introduced to help students acquire the language of role-plays and debates.

Page 7: Let's Debate!/Role-play! Groups now perform their role-play or hold a mini-debate, with two teams and a timekeeper. They are now combining information, opinions, key expressions and persuasion strategies, either in real-life role-play or in reasoned debate.

- **Opinion Samples:** These show how students can make role-play dialogues or debate arguments using the phrases from page 6. These samples are either on this or the following page.

Page 8: Reflection and Puzzle Page. The final page of each Unit offers students a chance to reflect on and review their learning. These activities take various forms in each Unit. In some, students are encouraged to reflect on their performance and achievement through self-assessments, surveys, or questionnaires. In others, Opinion Samples are followed by puzzles or riddles related to the topic of the Unit, encouraging students to engage in challenging, but creatively rewarding problem-solving.

Online Follow-up Activities. For teachers and students who want to do access reading, listening, viewing and other activities, suggested links to suitable online resources can be found on www.inkbooks.co.kr/.

In conclusion, I'd like to welcome you to this revised and expanded version of *Active English Discussion 1* and thank you for taking the time to read this preface. I sincerely hope it will provide endless opportunities for holistic development of discussion and debating skills, along with collaboration, respect, and the polite expression of opinions and ideas. Health and peace

Andrew Finch
November 2016

Contents

Preface	4
Who's Who	8

1 Names — 9
- What's in a name? — 10
- Discussion — 12
- Dialogue — 13
- Role-play — 14
- Samples and Review — 16

2 Pets — 17
- Man's Best Friend — 18
- Discussion — 20
- Dialogue — 21
- Role-play — 22
- Puzzle and Review — 24

3 Health — 25
- Healthy Body, Healthy Mind — 26
- Discussion — 28
- Dialogue — 29
- Role-play — 30
- Review — 32

4 Special Days — 33
- Important Days — 34
- Discussion — 36
- Dialogue — 37
- Role-play — 38
- Time to Create — 40

5 Role Models — 41
- Role Models — 42
- Discussion — 44
- Dialogue — 45
- Debate — 46
- Time to Think — 48

6 Family — 49
- The Korean Family — 50
- Discussion — 52
- Dialogue — 53
- Debate Tips — 54
- Reflection — 56

7 School Life — 57
- Learning by Doing — 58
- Discussion — 60
- Dialogue — 61
- Debate — 62

8 Sport — 65
- The Olympic Spirit — 66
- Discussion — 68
- Dialogue — 69
- Debate

9 Fashion — 73
- Eco-fashion — 74
- Discussion — 76
- Dialogue — 77
- Role-play — 78
- Reflection — 80

10 Dream Jobs — 81
- Right-brain Jobs — 82
- Discussion — 84
- Dialogue — 85
- Debate — 86
- Left/Right-brain Puzzle — 88

11 Well-being — 89
- Well-being School Lunches — 90
- Discussion — 92
- Dialogue — 93
- Role-play — 94
- Brainteasers and Reflection — 96

12 Travel in Korea — 97
- Travel in Korea — 98
- Discussion — 100
- Dialogue — 101
- Debate — 102
- Reflection — 104

13 Myths — 105
- Creation Myths — 106
- Discussion — 108
- Dialogue — 109
- Action Stories — 110
- My Speaking Skills — 112

14 Smart Technology — 113
- Smart phones — 114
- Discussion — 116
- Dialogue — 117
- Debate — 118
- Reflection — 120

15 Water — 121
- Water Shortage — 122
- Discussion — 124
- Dialogue — 125
- Mock Trial — 126
- Tips and Bridge Puzzle — 128

16 Television — 129
- Viewing Habits — 130
- Discussion — 132
- Dialogue — 133
- Debate — 134
- Puzzle — 136

17 Success and Happiness — 137
- Happiness — 138
- Discussion — 140
- Dialogue — 141
- Success Interview — 142
- Self-assessment — 144

18 Learning for Life — 145
- What Do You See? — 146
- Discussion — 148
- Dialogue — 149
- Trivia Game — 150
- Review — 152

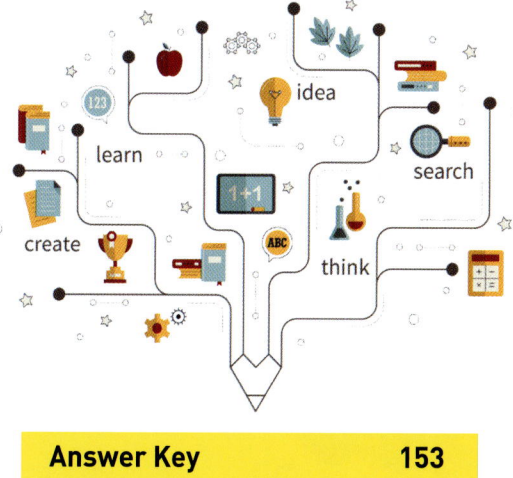

Answer Key — 153

Website: www.inkbooks.co.kr

Who's Who?

Family and Friends

- We're going to meet six people in this book.
- They will talk about the topics in each unit.
- Can you find out who they are?
➡ Write their names in the empty spaces.

This is Michael's mother. She is called _ _ _ _ _ _ _.

Grandma Brown's son is called _ _ _ _ _ _.

_ _ _ _ _ is Michael's wife.

This is Kevin's friend, Park _ _ _ _ _ _-_ _ _.

Kim _ _-_ _ _ is Jenny's friend.

Jenny's brother, _ _ _ _ _, is Seung-min's friend.

_ _ _ _ _ is Helen's daughter and Ji-hye's friend.

*You can check the names in the Answer Section at the back of the book.

1 Names

Brainstorming

- What do you know about your name? What does it mean?
- What are the most popular names in your country?

Task 1
- Look at this table. Talk about it with your partner.
- Can you guess the top boys' and girls' names in the USA, the UK and Korea?
- Write ①, ②, ③, ④, ⑤ next to the names.

The answers are in the Answer Key at the back of the book.

Most Popular Baby Names in 2015

USA		UK		Korea	
girls	boys	girls	boys	girls	boys
Amelia	③ Jack	Amelia	Charlie	Ji-u	Ju-won
Emily	Jacob	④ Emily	Harry	Min-seo	Min-jun
Lily	Muhammad	Isla	② Jack	Seo-hyeon	Seo-jun
① Olivia	Noah	Olivia	Jacob	Seo-yeon	Si-u
Sophia	Oliver	Poppy	Oliver	Seo-yun	Ye-jun

Here are some of these names and their meanings:

Noah	→	Comfort, rest	Olivia	→	Olive, peace
Harry	→	Army commander	Sophia	→	Wisdom
Charlie	→	Manly	Isla	→	Island
Muhammad	→	Praised	Emily	→	Industrious

Task 2
- Ask people about their names.

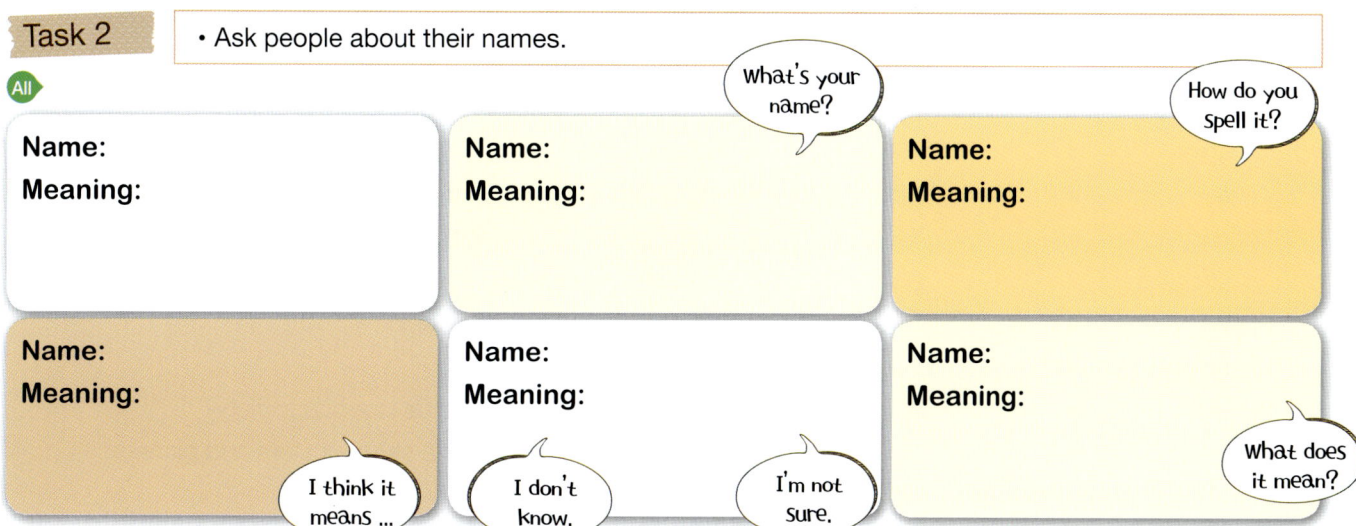

What's in a name?

- Listen to Track 1 on the CD-Rom.
- Read this passage about 'names' together.
- While you read, match the words and phrases at the bottom of the page.
- Then answer the questions on the next page.

 Groups

Do you think your name affects your personality? If you were called Kevin, would you be kind, gentle, and handsome, just like the meaning of your name? Or if you were called Jenny, would you be like a fair spirit or a white wave?

Imagine you are choosing a name for your baby. What name will you choose, and how will you choose it? Do you want a fashionable or a traditional name for your baby? Will you search on the Internet for the most popular baby names? Each culture has its favorite names and naming-customs, so here are some from around the world.

Mongolian names have beautiful sounds and meanings, such as *Bayaarm*: "Mother of Joy." If you watch the movie *Dancing with Wolves* (1990), you will see that North American Indian names like *Chilam* (Snow Bird) and *Demothi* (Talks while Walking) describe what the mother saw when the baby was born. Eskimo babies are named by the elders, while in Russia long ago, you could tell someone's occupation and family relationship from their name. For example, "portnoi" means "tailor" and "ova" means "daughter." So "Portnova" means "Daughter of the Tailor."

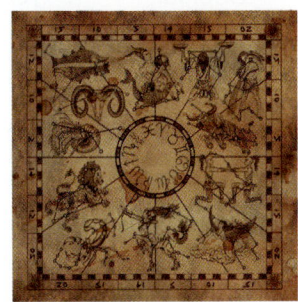

Many people believe the stars and planets are important influences, so they look for astrological baby names, based on the Zodiac sign of the baby's day of birth. All in all, there are many things to think about when naming your child.

Match the words and phrases on the left to the definitions on the right.

culture	a job, career
custom	a large object which goes round the sun
elder	a pattern of life passed from one generation to another
occupation	a person who makes and repairs clothes
relationship	a senior, respected, aged person
tailor	connection between people
astrology	help to change, affect
planet	the arts, beliefs, and behaviors of a society
influence	telling the future from the study of stars and planets

There are more reading passages at www.inkbooks.co.kr

10 Active English Discussion 1

Comprehension Check

1. Do people in different cultures use the same names?
2. Where is Mongolia?
   ☐ South America   ☐ Asia   ☐ Africa   ☐ Europe
3. How do American Indian women choose their babies' names?
4. If *Pastukh* means 'shepherd,' what does *Pastukhova* mean?
5. What is the difference between the Western Zodiac and the Oriental Zodiac?
6. Why do people think of the stars and planets when choosing a baby's name?
7. This passage explains the best method of giving a name to a baby.   ☐ True   ☐ False

Think for Yourself

☐ How was your name chosen? Who chose it?
☐ If you could change your name, what would you choose?
  • What would it mean?
  • Why would you choose it?

Background Information

Miller   Smith   Baker   Tailor

Did you know?

☐ In Ethiopia, your father's first name becomes your last name.
   For example, If your father is called Birhanu Tesfay, your name could be Demesie Birhanu, and your child could be called Bein Demesie.

☐ In Wales, people used to be called by their occupations. For example: Evans the Bread (Baker) and Jones the Milk (Milkman).

☐ In England and the USA, many family names still refer to the ancestors' occupations. For example: Albert Miller, George Smith, Terry Baker, Alice Tailor and John Nobleman.

☐ The names of the royal princes (Harry, George, and William) ranked 3rd, 7th and 10th as baby names in the UK in 2015.

☐ In Portugal, people can have two, three or more family names.
   For example: José Eduardo Santos Tavares Melo Silva.
       (given names) (mother's names) (father's family names).

Discussion Us Groups

- Talk to each other about these questions.
- Use the Conversation Strategies at the bottom of the page.

1. Are you proud of your name?
   - Why? Why not? Support your opinion.

2. Does your name affect your personality?
   - Please explain.

3. Is it OK to 'Westernize' your name?
   - (e.g. Ji-hye Kim instead of Kim Ji-hye)

4. Is it OK to have a western nickname?

5. What name would you give to your son or daughter?
   - How would you choose the name?

6. Would you let your elders choose your child's name?
   - Why? Why not? Support your opinion.

7. Why do you think people change their names?
   - Can you think of any famous people who changed their names?
   - Would you like to change your name?
   - Why? Why not?

8. What do you think about astrology?
   - Would you ask a name-maker to name your child?
   - Why? Why not? Support your opinion.

Conversation Strategies

Asking for Information:
Excuse me …
Can I ask a question?
Do you know …?
Can you tell me …?
I'd like to know …
Pardon me for asking, but …

Making sure:
What did you say?
Pardon?
How do you spell it?
What does it mean?
Can you say that again?
One more time, please.

Dialogue

- Listen to Track 2 on the CD-Rom.
- Read the dialogue with your partner.
- Perform the dialogue together.
- Change roles. Perform the dialogue again.

Ji-hye	Hi, Kevin. What are you reading?
Kevin	Well, … do you know what a biography is, Ji-hye?
Ji-hye	Let me think. Isn't it the story of someone's life?
Kevin	Yes, it is. This one is about Muhammed Ali, the heavyweight boxer.
Ji-hye	He threw his Olympic Gold Medal into a river, didn't he?
Kevin	That's right. He's a legend in his time.
Ji-hye	He wasn't always called Muhammed Ali, though, was he?
Kevin	No. He changed his name from Cassius Clay.
Ji-hye	Is that the man who said "I have a dream"?
Kevin	No. That was Martin Luther King.
Ji-hye	Oh, yes. Why did Cassius change his name?
Kevin	He became a Muslim, so he wanted to make a new start.
Ji-hye	That explains it. I've heard that he was a man of peace.

Key Words and Expressions

biography
a book about the life of a famous person

a legend in his/her time
someone who is very famous during his/her lifetime

make a new start
begin a new life, leaving the old one behind

"That explains it."
"I understand." "That makes sense."

man of peace
a person whose whole life is about peace

Tag questions
"didn't he?" "was he?"

Dialogue Quiz

1. What is the difference between an autobiography and a biography?
2. What was Muhammed Ali's original name?
3. Why did he change his name?
4. Why did he throw his gold medal into a river?
5. Which river was it?

Let's Make a Role-play! Groups

Situation: There are four people in your family: Grandfather, mother, father, and daughter.
Very soon there will be a new addition: a newborn baby. You are going to discuss how to choose a new name for him or her.

Track 3 to 6

1. Choose your role (grandfather, mother, father or daughter).
2. Read your role-card and the opinion sample.
3. Think about what you will say in the role-play.
4. Write your ideas on the mind-map on the next page.

Grandfather: You want to go to a fortune-teller. Here is your opinion sample:

Why not let the stars and planets decide the baby's name? There are many things in life that we can't understand, but that doesn't mean they're wrong. Our ancestors were in tune with nature and the seasons. They could forecast the weather, even without satellites. I want to ask an astrologer to choose a lucky name, just like my ancestors did.

Mother: You want to name the baby yourself. Here is your opinion sample:

Elders and fortune tellers know about tradition and customs, but they're not up-to-date. They don't understand how quickly the world is changing. A traditional name can sound old-fashioned now, so I want to search the Internet for baby names. I will look at baby sites and find names that are most popular in my country.

Father: You want to choose a traditional name. Here is your opinion sample:

My father chose my name, so I want to choose my son's name. He will carry on my bloodline, so he needs a traditional name that has been in the family for generations. I will ask my father for advice. He knows all the most respected names in our family. I don't like these modern, trendy names. They go out of date very quickly.

Daughter: You want to choose a fashionable name. Here is your opinion sample:

I want to give the baby a wonderful, fashionable name. If it is a girl we can name it after a famous singer. Or if it is a boy, we can name it after a famous footballer or baseball player. I also think children should choose their names when they grow up. Till then, they can be called "son of ..." or "daughter of ..." as in Russia and other countries.

My Mind-map

- Fill in the mind-map with your ideas for the role-play.

My opinion:

Great names for boys:

Baby names

Great names for girls:

Let's begin!

- Use these phrases when you perform your role play.

That's true.

I agree with you.

You have a good point.

That's an idea!

I don't agree with you.

I don't agree, because...

You may be right, but ...

That's a great idea!

I don't think that's a very good idea.

Can I make a suggestion?

I can't agree with you.

What do you think?

When you have finished, complete this final statement about your discussion:

We have agreed that if the baby is a boy it will be called _____.

On the other hand, if the baby is a girl, it will be called _____.

Signed: 1. _____ 2. _____ 3. _____ 4. _____

Unit 1 Names 15

Time to Think! Us 2

- Look at these puzzles with a partner and see if you can solve them.
- The answers are at the back of the book.

1. Michael's mother (Grandma Brown) has 4 children. Three are named George, Susan and Emily. What is the 4th child's name?

2. Sam, Jenny, Peter, James and Lily have different family names. Can you find out what they are? Here are some clues:

   - James' family name does not have 3 or 4 letters.
   - Peter's family name does not have a "n" in it.
   - Sam's family name has no "e".
   - Lily's family name does not end in "n".

3. You are my brother, but I am not your brother. Who am I?

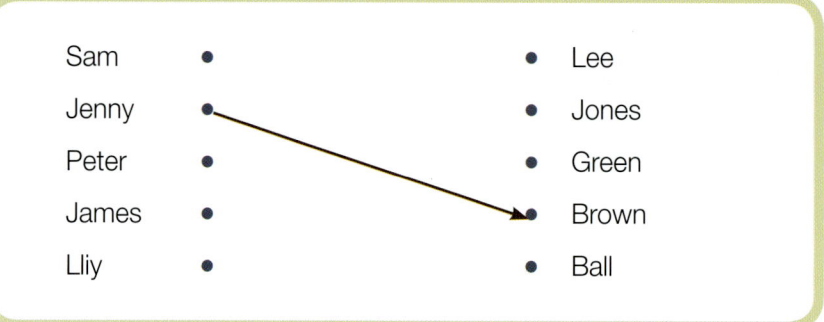

Reflect and Review

- How did you do in this Unit?

How was your speaking (pages 9, 12, 15)?			
Great	Good	OK	Could be better
How was your reading (pages 10, 13, 14)?			
Great	Good	OK	Could be better
How was your team work with your group and your partner?			
Great	Good	OK	Could be better
Did you learn any new words, idioms, or phrases? What were they?			
How about looking at the online activities for this Unit? www.inkbooks.co.kr			

2 Pets

Task 1

- Fill in this chart with your partner.

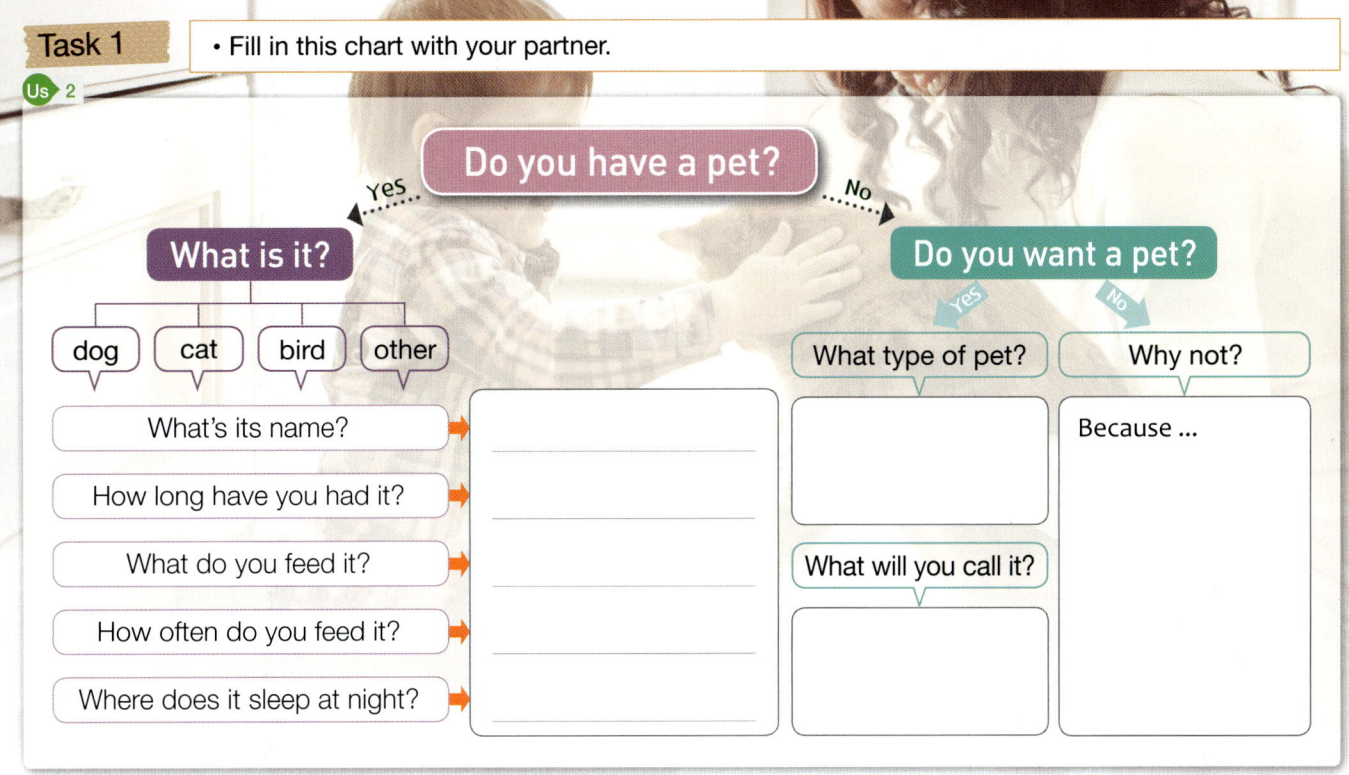

Do you have a pet?

Yes → **What is it?**
- dog / cat / bird / other
- What's its name?
- How long have you had it?
- What do you feed it?
- How often do you feed it?
- Where does it sleep at night?

No → **Do you want a pet?**

Yes → What type of pet? / What will you call it?

No → Why not? Because …

Task 2

Us > Groups

- How many types of pets can you think of?
- What are the good things about pets?
- Are there any problems with pets?
- Share your ideas and write them in the boxes below.

Types of pets

Good things about pets
I like pets because …

Problems with pets
The problem is … You have to …

Unit 2 Pets 17

Man's Best Friend

- Listen to Track 7 on the CD-Rom.
- Read this passage together.
- While you read, match the words and phrases at the bottom of the page.
- Then answer the questions on the next page.

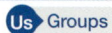 Groups

Cropper is the perfect pet. He is friendly, loyal, and likes to be stroked. But he is a fox! In Britain, foxes are pests. They raid trash bins, dig up flower beds, make a home under garden sheds, and kill pet rabbits and guinea pigs. However, Cropper is different. He was badly injured in a fight and was rescued by the Fox Project in Tunbridge Wells. His new owner took care of him and gained his trust and friendship. Now Cropper behaves just like a dog.

What do you think of this news item? Can a fox really be a pet? Exotic pets such as spiders, snakes, frogs, crabs, and insects are becoming more and more popular in the west these days. In fact, according to CNN, "More tigers are kept as pets in the U.S. than roam free in the wild."

Wolves were probably the first animals to be domesticated, more than 10,000 years ago. Since then, their descendants have become 'man's best friend'. Not only are dogs good pets, but they also guide blind people and help the police. Cats have been around for a long time as well. They were sacred animals in Egypt, where the cat-goddess Bast was worshipped from 3,200 BCE.

Doctors often prescribe "therapy animals" to people in hospitals, retirement homes, and disaster areas. These animals are trained to give comfort to those who need exercise, fresh air, and companionship. So as we can see, pets give friendship and joy to many people around the world. If they are given a good home, they can be like one of the family.

Match the words to their definitions.

loyal	an animal or insect that causes problems for humans
pest	children, offspring
injure	holy, divine
exotic	to hurt, damage, cause harm
prescribe	to tell someone to use medicine or therapy
therapy	to tame a wild animal to live with humans
domesticate	special treatment for an illness
descendants	trustworthy, faithful
sacred	unusual or strange in appearance

Comprehension Check

1. What do people in Britain usually think of foxes?
2. How is Cropper different from other foxes?
3. How did Cropper meet his owner?
4. What are therapy animals? What are they used for?
5. What were dogs before they were domesticated?
6. How do dogs help humans?
7. Why were cats holy animals in Egypt?
8. What is the modern role of pets?

Think for Yourself

- [ ] Can you think of any holy animals?
- [ ] Do you know any animals that help humans?
- [ ] If you could be a pet, what would you choose to be?
    - I would like to be: _____
- [ ] There are many animal charities. What do these letters stand for?
    - RSPCA _____
    - RSPB _____
    - WWF _____
    - PAWS _____

Background Information

Did you know?

- [ ] The dog, Laikia, was the first living creature to go into space. She went round the earth in a Russian satellite in 1957.
- [ ] Two dogs survived the wreck of the Titanic.
- [ ] Pigeons can find their way home from long distances. Birds which have been taken 2,500 kms from home have still found their way back safely.
- [ ] There are approximately 78 million dogs in the USA and 86 million cats.
- [ ] More than half of the families in the USA (61 million) have pets.
- [ ] People who own pets experience less stress, have fewer heart attacks, and live longer.
- [ ] Americans spend more money on pets each year than on beer and movies.

Discussion Us Groups

- Talk about the questions below.
- Use the Conversation Strategies at the bottom of the page.

1. **Have you ever owned a pet?**
   - Talk about the advantages and disadvantages.

2. **Would you like to be a pet?**
   - Why? Why not?

3. **Can pets think? Do they understand humans?**
   - Explain your opinion.

4. **Do pets have emotions? Can they feel happy or sad?**
   - Explain your opinion.

5. **Do pets have souls?**
   - Please explain your opinion.

6. **Would you give a pet as a present to someone?**
   - Why? Why not?

7. **Is it OK to have pets when many people in the world are starving?**
   - Explain and support your opinion.

8. **Why is it OK to eat some animals, but not pets?**
   - What do you think about vegetarians and vegans?

9. **Do animals have legal rights?**
   - Should they have the same basic rights as humans?

10. **Is it OK to use animals for testing cosmetics?**
    - Is it OK to use animals for testing medicines?

Conversation Strategies

Agreeing:	Bringing someone into the discussion:
I agree.	How about you?
That's right.	What do you think?
Exactly!	How do you feel?
That's a good point.	Do you agree?
You said it!	Don't you agree?
Tell me about it.	Tell us your opinion.

Dialogue

- Listen to Track 8 on the CD-Rom.
- Read the dialogue with your partner.
- Perform the dialogue together.
- Change roles. Perform the dialogue again.

(Jenny is calling to a dog.)

Jenny	C'mon, c'mon. … Come to Jenny. … Here, Stranger.
Seung-min	Hey, Jenny. What's new?
Jenny	Hi, Seung-min. Meet my new pet. I've called it "Stranger."
Seung-min	I didn't know you liked dogs. Was it a birthday present?
Jenny	No. It's a stray. It followed me home from the park.
Seung-min	Really? Does it have a name tag on its collar?
Jenny	No. I've looked. It's all by itself, with no home to go to.
Seung-min	We should tell the police. Its owner could be looking for it.
Jenny	But it's so sweet. Look at it wagging its tail!
Seung-min	Come on, Jenny. Some poor girl could be crying her eyes out right now.
Jenny	OK. I suppose you're right.
Seung-min	Maybe if it hasn't been reported missing, you can keep it.
Jenny	Do you think so? Oh, I wish …

Key Words and Expressions

"What's new?"
"What's happening?" "Is there anything interesting to tell me?"

stray
an animal with no owner and no home

name tag
a card with the animal's name and address

wagging its tail
moving its tail up and down and side to side

crying her eyes out
unable to stop crying

"I wish …"
"If only ……";
"I hope that will happen."

Dialogue Quiz

1. Why do you think Jenny called the dog 'Stranger'?
2. Do you think Jenny will keep the dog?
3. There are many abandoned animals in the world. How about in your country?
4. Why do people abandon animals?
5. What is an animal shelter?
6. Would you like to adopt a pet from an animal shelter?

Let's Make a Role-play! Groups

Situation: Jenny has taken the dog home. She asks Michael, Helen and Kevin whether she can have it as a pet. You are going to discuss whether to keep 'Stranger' or send it to an animal shelter.

Track 9 to 12

1. Choose your role (Michael, Helen, Jenny or Kevin).
2. Read your role-card and the opinion sample.
3. Listen to Tracks 9 to 12 on the Audio CD-Rom.
4. Think about what you will say in the role-play.
5. Write your ideas on the mind-map on the next page.

Jenny: You want to keep Stranger as a pet. Here is your opinion sample:

I love dogs and I have always wanted one of my own. I promise to look after Stranger and take care of him. I will play with him and take him to the park every day. He is so cute, I know we will be great friends. All my friends have pets, so I really want to have one too.

Michael: You think pets are too much trouble. Here is your opinion sample:

Pets are lovely for a short time. But you have to look after them every day. They make a mess and they need to be trained to obey you. Who will look after Stranger when Helen and I are at work and Jenny and Kevin are at school? Who will take him to the vet when he is sick? I think we should take this dog to the Dog Shelter.

Kevin: You don't like pets. Here is your opinion sample:

It seems to me that people think more of their pets than they do of other human beings. Whenever I go to the park, I see dogs everywhere. People spend too much on cat food and dog food and they treat their pets like members of the family. I wish they would spend that money on homeless, sick and elderly people.

Helen: You want Jenny to look after Stranger. Here is your opinion sample:

We all need to share love, and pets are perfect for this. They are always ready to have a cuddle and play games. Of course, Jenny must promise to look after Stranger. She must feed him, train him to be clean and give him regular exercise. She should not expect me to do these things for her, even when she is very busy.

My Mind-map

- Fill in the mind-map with your ideas for the role-play.

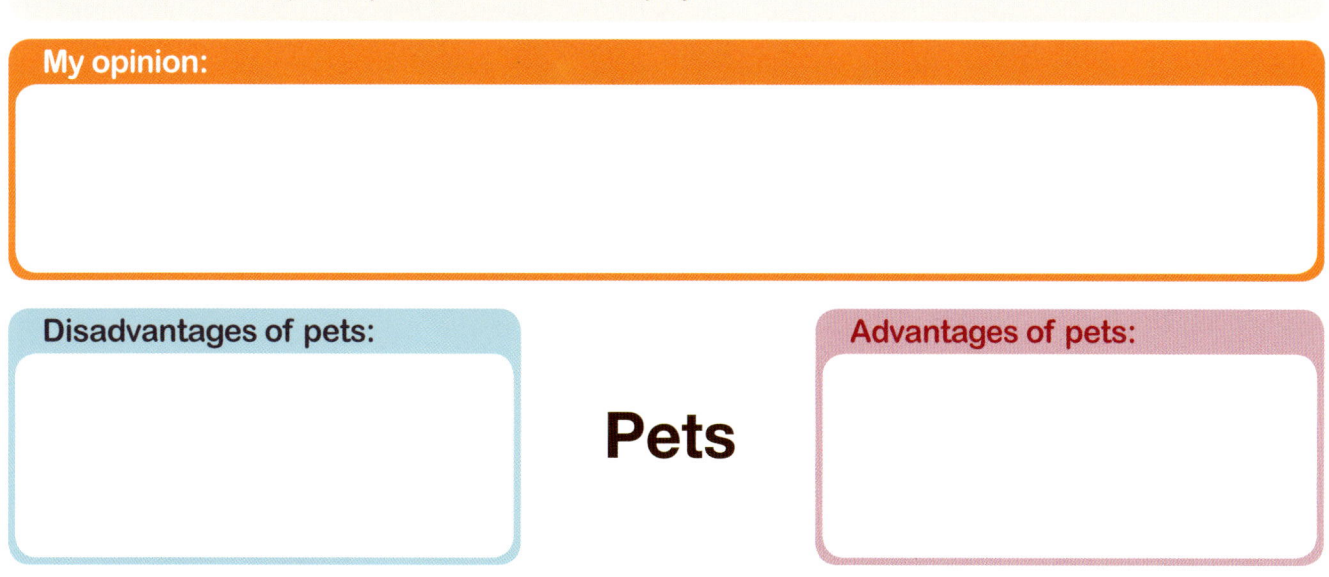

Let's begin!

- Use these phrases when you perform your role-play.

When you have finished, complete this final statement about your discussion:

We have agreed that Jenny can/cannot keep Stranger.

Signed: 1. _____   2. _____   3. _____   4. _____

Time to Think!

• Look at these riddles with a partner and see if you can solve them.

1. What type of dog keeps the best time?
   _____

2. What happens when it rains cats and dogs?
   _____

3. When is a black cat bad luck?
   _____

4. What is cat's favorite song?
   _____

5. Why do hummingbirds hum?
   _____

6. Why do birds fly south for the winter?
   _____

The answers are in the Answer Section at the back of the book.

Reflect and Review

• How did you do in this Unit?

How was my speaking (pages 17, 20, 23)?			
Great	Good	OK	Poor (I will do my best.)
How was my reading (pages 18, 21, 22)?			
Great	Good	OK	Poor (I will do my best.)
How was my team work with my group and my partner?			
Great	Good	OK	Poor (I will do my best.)
Did I learn any new words, idioms, or phrases? What were they?			
How about looking at the online activities for this Unit? www.inkbooks.co.kr			

3 Health

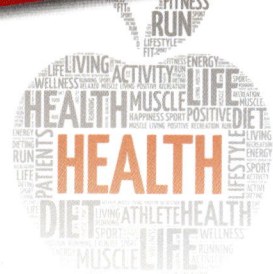

Task 1
- Imagine you can do anything you want to do this weekend.
- Choose the top 5 things you want to do.
- Write 1, 2, 3, 4, 5 below.

This weekend, I want to …

___ do aerobics	___ do yoga	___ go dancing	___ go for a swim
___ go hiking	___ go jogging	___ go inline skating	___ go shopping
___ go to a movie	___ hangout	___ have a date	___ listen to music
___ play basketball	___ play computer games	___ play piano	___ play soccer
___ read a book	___ ride my bike	___ study English	___ watch television

Task 2
- Talk to people in the class. What do they want to do this weekend?
- When you find someone who says "Yes, I do", write his or her name in the box.
- How many boxes can you fill?

Excuse me. Can I ask you a question? Do you want to …? ▶ Yes, I do./ No, I don't.
Do you mind if I ask you something? Do you want to …? ▶ Yes, I do. /No, I don't.

Find someone who wants to play computer games.	Find someone who wants to watch television.	Find someone who wants to play basketball.	Find someone who wants to listen to music.
Name:	Name:	Name:	Name:
Find someone who wants to read a book.	Find someone who wants to do yoga.	Find someone who wants to ride a bike.	Find someone who wants to go dancing.
Name:	Name:	Name:	Name:
Find someone who wants to go hiking.	Find someone who wants to go skating.	Find someone who wants to go jogging.	Find someone who wants to hangout.
Name:	Name:	Name:	Name:
Find someone who wants to go to a movie.	Find someone who wants to do aerobics.	Find someone who wants to play piano.	Find someone who wants to play soccer.
Name:	Name:	Name:	Name:
Find someone who wants to have a date.	Find someone who wants to go shopping.	Find someone who wants to go for a swim.	Find someone who wants to study English.
Name:	Name:	Name:	Name:

Healthy Mind, Healthy Body

- Listen to Track 13 on the CD-Rom.
- Read this passage together.
- While you read, match the words and phrases at the bottom of the page.
- Then answer the questions on the next page.

 Groups

Can you answer this riddle?

> I am the most precious thing in the world.
> You can't buy me in a shop or give me as a present.
> I don't grow on trees, and you can't eat me.
> Everybody wants to keep me forever.
> Everybody has me, but they sometimes lose me.
> What am I?

Did you guess? Yes, the answer is 'health.' Health is the most valuable thing we have. If we lose it, then money and possessions are useless. The strange thing is that we often take it for granted. We don't think about our health until it has gone. Then we realize how important it is.

Have you ever thought about your body? It's a wonderful collection of parts, all working together. The heart sends blood round the body, and the lungs take in air. Your stomach digests food, and sends it to the muscles. The bones let you run, walk, dance, and play. Your brain has thoughts and ideas. Scientists have studied our bodies and brains for some time, in order to make robots and clones. Yet every new baby has a body which grows by itself, as if it knows what to do.

The body needs exercise to stay healthy, but these days, people spend their time in schools, offices, cars, or in front of the television. Because of this, the body runs down, becoming tired and sick. We need to eat wisely and exercise regularly in order to live a happy and healthy life.

Match the words and phrases on the left to the definitions on the right.

riddle	a group of objects
precious	an exact copy
possessions	goods, money, belongings
take for granted	of great value, dearly loved
collection	organs which give oxygen to the body
lungs	puzzle, brain-teaser
digest	to accept without question, ignore
clone	to become worn out, unwell
run down	to take food into the body

There are more reading passages at www.inkbooks.co.kr

Comprehension Check

1. Can you find another word that means 'precious' in this passage?
2. 'Everybody has me, but they sometimes lose me.' What does this mean?
3. Why do we often take health for granted?
4. How does oxygen get into the body?
5. Can scientists make a human body?
6. Why do people get less exercise these days?
7. How can we have a healthy lifestyle?

Think for Yourself

- [ ] Do you know any riddles?
- [ ] Try this one:

> I'm as small as an ant, and as big as a whale.
> People can hit me, but they can't hurt me.
> I dance to the music, though I can't hear.
> You can't run away from me. What am I?
> *The answer is in the Answer Key, at the back of the book.

Background Information

Here are 10 ways to keep fit:

1. Wear comfortable shoes. Walk at least 30 minutes every day.
2. If you want to talk to a friend or a neighbor, how about taking a walk? Use your legs instead of the telephone.
3. Eat a healthy breakfast. This is the most important meal, getting you ready for the whole day.
4. Climbing stairs is great exercise, and it's free! Use your legs instead of the elevator.
5. Drink at least 8 glasses of water a day. Water is essential for every living thing. Our bodies are 60% water.
6. Do some stretching and deep breathing during the day. This helps to get oxygen to your body.
7. Eat fruits and vegetables. They contain nutrients and vitamins that are important for your health.
8. Spend at least 30 minutes outdoors. Sunlight helps us in many ways. A walk in the fresh air is a good way of keeping fit.
9. Make some quiet time for yourself. Sitting quietly for a short time helps us to calm down and release stress.
10. Keep regular sleep hours. This gives your body a natural rhythm, which helps it to stay healthy.

Discussion Groups

- Talk about the questions below.
- Use the Conversation Strategies at the bottom of the page.

1. Which is more important, health, money, or love?
   - Explain your opinion.

2. How can we be healthy and happy?
   - Explain your opinion.

3. 'An apple a day keeps the doctor away.'
   - Do you know any proverbs like this?
   - What sort of foods should we eat?
   - What sort of foods shouldn't we eat?

4. Do Vitamin pills help us to stay healthy?
   - Why? Why not? Support your opinion.

5. Have you heard of 'health freaks' and 'couch potatoes'?
   - How much exercise should we do?
   - What? Where? How often?

6. Have you ever been admitted to hospital?
   - Yes? Tell us about it.
   - No? Have you ever visited anyone in hospital?

7. Do you prefer western medicine or oriental medicine?
   - Explain your opinion.

8. "Mens Sana in Corpore Sano" – A Healthy Mind in a Healthy Body
   - What does this mean to you? Do you agree with it?

Conversation Strategies

Disagreeing:	Making sure:
I'm not sure I agree.	Right?
I don't think so.	OK so far?
I can't agree.	Is that clear?
I disagree.	Have you got it?
No way!	Do you follow me?
You must be joking!	Are you with me?
You're pulling my leg!	Do you understand?

Dialogue

- Read this dialogue.
- Listen to Track 14 on the CD-Rom.
- Perform the dialogue together.
- Change roles. Perform the dialogue again.

Kevin	Bye, Mum.
Mum	Where're you off to, Kevin?
Kevin	The gym, of course. You know I go there every Saturday.
Mum	Have a good time, then. *(Kevin leaves)*
Jenny	I really don't get Kevin.
Mum	Why's that, Jenny?
Jenny	He's always exercising, or playing some sport or other. I wouldn't go to the gym, even if you paid me.
Mum	So what? He likes to keep fit.
Jenny	I know, but he's a fitness freak. It's all he thinks about.
Mum	Isn't that better than being a couch potato?
Jenny	What do you mean?
Mum	Maybe you should do something active, too.
Jenny	Oh yeah? And how would I study for my exams?
Mum	Regular exercise gives you more energy for studying, Jen. I thought you knew that.

Key Words and Expressions

"I really don't get Kevin."
"I don't understand Kevin."

"So what?"
"What's the problem?"
"What's wrong with that?"

keep fit
stay healthy through exercise

"I wouldn't … even if you paid me."
"There's no way I would do that."

Dialogue Quiz

1. How often does Kevin go to the gym?
2. Why doesn't Jenny do something active?
3. Is Jenny a couch potato?
4. How will exercise help Jenny?
5. Who do you think Mum agrees with?
6. Where are you on this line?

Fitness freak ←————————→ **Couch potato**

Let's Make a Role-play! Groups

Situation: You are taking part in a TV chat-show. Today's topic is 'How to live a healthy life.' On today's panel are Mr. Fitness Freak, Ms. Couch Potato and A. Student. They are introduced by the Host.

1. Choose your role. Then read your role-card and your hints.
2. Think about what you will say in the role-play.
3. Write your ideas on the next page.

TV Show Host

Here are your hints:

1. Greet the viewers.
2. Introduce tonight's panel members.
3. Say something about each person.
4. Start the discussion.
5. Ask a question to each panel member.
6. Make sure everyone speaks an equal amount of time.
7. Close the show.
8. Tell the viewers how to live a healthy life.
9. Say goodbye.

Here are some useful phrases:

- Good evening everyone.
- Tonight we will be discussing ....
- We have some special guests tonight.
- Let me ask you a question.
- What do you think?
- How about you?
- It's time to finish.
- Goodbye and thanks for viewing.
- Next week we will be discussing ...

Mr. Fitness Freak, Ms. Couch Potato, and A. Student

Here are your hints:

Thank the Host for inviting you tonight.
Tell the host your ideas for living a healthy life.
Explain your opinion.
Agree or disagree with the other panel members.
Try to make a final agreement with everyone.

Look at pages 23 and 28 for some useful conversation strategies. Here are some more that you can use:

I'd just like to say that ...
Second, ... third, ... finally, ...
I see your point, but ...
In conclusion ...
On the one hand ...
On the other hand ...
To sum up, ...
Can I say something?
First of all, ...
I see what you mean.
In my opinion, ...
I think that ...

My Ideas

- Make notes about how to live a healthy life (according to your role-play character).

First of all, ...
_____
_____
_____

Second, ...
_____
_____
_____

Third, ...
_____
_____
_____

Finally, ...
_____
_____
_____

Opinion Samples

- Here are two samples to give you some ideas.

Opinion 1: First of all, I don't believe in keeping fit. In my opinion it's all a waste of time. I don't do any exercise, but I'm never sick. Second, I eat what I want to eat, and I do what I want to do. It doesn't seem to make any difference. Third, I think that health is in the mind. If you're always looking for problems and worrying about tomorrow, you get sick. To sum up, I just take tomorrow as it comes.

Opinion 2: I'd just like to say that it's easy to ignore health, especially for young people. They think they will always be healthy, so they eat junk food and skip meals. Later, they find they can't take health for granted any more. I'm not going to be like that. I want to take care of my body, so that I can enjoy every moment of my life. I eat healthily and I lead an active lifestyle. I'm not sacrificing tomorrow to the bad habits of today.

Time to Think!

- Here is a questionnaire. Choose your answers and find your 'healthy living' score.

1. Before I go out in the sun I put on sunscreen, clothing and a hat.					
	Always	Often	Sometimes	Rarely	Never
2. I protect my skin even in winter and on cloudy days.					
	Always	Often	Sometimes	Rarely	Never
3. I stay away from smokers' second-hand smoke.					
	Always	Often	Sometimes	Rarely	Never
4. I exercise to keep my body fit.					
	Always	Often	Sometimes	Rarely	Never
5. I am active in my daily life.					
	Always	Often	Sometimes	Rarely	Never
6. I include vegetables, nuts and fruit in my diet.					
	Always	Often	Sometimes	Rarely	Never
7. I stay away from junk food, fast food, or sugary drinks.					
	Always	Often	Sometimes	Rarely	Never
8. When I eat out, I look for healthy dishes on the menu.					
	Always	Often	Sometimes	Rarely	Never
9. I spend less than 2 hours watching TV, surfing the Internet, or playing computer games.					
	Always	Often	Sometimes	Rarely	Never
10. I get 7 or 8 hours sleep at night.					
	Always	Often	Sometimes	Rarely	Never

Always = 4 points, Often = 3 points, sometimes = 2, rarely = 1, never = 0

I scored _____ out of 40 points.

Reflect and Review

- What do you think about your score? How can you become more healthy?

I need to _____

It would be a good idea to _____

I should start _____

I should stop _____

4 Special Days

Brainstorming
- Let's find out about some special days around the world.

Task 1
- Match the special days to their descriptions.

April Fool's Day	Families come together at this time and give thanks for a fruitful year.
Arbor Day	On this day, people who didn't get gifts on Valentine's Day or White Day eat noodles with black bean sauce.
Black Day	Servants received Christmas Boxes from their masters and poor boxes in churches were opened on this day.
Boxing Day	During the morning, people play jokes on friends and family. But if you play a joke in the afternoon, you are the fool.
Chuseok	This day celebrates the making of the Korean alphabet by King Sejong the Great.
Hangul Day	When this special day was first observed in 1872, more than 1 million trees were planted.
St. Patrick's Day	On this holiday, people wear green clothes, eat Irish food, drink green drinks and watch parades.

*The answers are in the Answer Key, at the back of the book.

Task 2
- How many special days can you think of?
- Write the names in the table below.

National Holidays	Public Holidays	Other Special Days
Independence Day	New Year's Day	Arbor Day

Important Days

- Listen to Track 17 on the CD-Rom.
- Read this passage together.
- While you read, match the words and phrases at the bottom of the page.
- Then answer the questions on the next page.

 Groups

Did you know that there are 23 Special Days each year in Korea, of which 17 are National Holidays? These traditional festivals commemorate religious, national, and international events. However, lots of other special days have also appeared in recent years. Here are some examples.

March 8 is International Women's Day, when we think of women's roles in society. We also remember women who changed the world, like Emmeline Pankhurst, Marie Curie, Helen Keller and Mother Teresa. The 22nd of the next month is Earth Day, when people around the world call for environmental protection. Later in the year, International Day of Peace (September 21) is followed by Native American Day, on the fourth Friday of September.

HUANG Zheng / Shutterstock.com

Closer to home, Random Acts of Kindness Day (September 1) and Buy Nothing Day (November 26) speak to us about our own lives. The first of these encourages us to be kind to everyone. The second has the motto "Shop Less, Live More" and challenges us to go for 24 hours without spending any money.

All these days remind us of important issues in our modern lives and help us think about how to make the world a better place. Can you find any more special days like these?

Match the words and phrases to their definitions.

traditional	to say that something must happen
religious	the part played by someone in a family or society
commemorate	the natural world
role	reminding people of an important event
call for	relating to belief in a god or gods
environment	make us more determined; advise
protection	keeping from harm or loss
closer to home	involving us directly
encourage	invite someone to do something difficult
challenge	an established way of doing things

There are more reading passages at www.inkbooks.co.kr

Comprehension Check

1. How many special days in Korea are not National Holidays?
2. How did Emmeline Pankhurst change the world?
3. How did Marie Curie change the world?
4. How about Helen Keller and Mother Teresa?
5. What do you think happens on Native American Day?
6. Why is Native American Day important?
7. What does "Shop Less, Live More" mean?

Think for Yourself

- ☐ If you could make your own Special Day, what would you call it?
- ☐ What date would it fall on? What would you celebrate?

  • My Special Day would be called: _____

  • It would fall on: _____

  • It would celebrate: _____

Background Information

Did you know?

- ☐ Here are some Special Days.
- ☐ Do you know what they commemorate?

Black Day	Halloween	Remembrance Day
Buddha's Birthday	Hanukkah	Solar New Year
Children's Day	Hungry Ghost Day	Teachers' Day
Christmas Day	Independence Day	Thanksgiving Day
Diwali	Labor Day	United Nations Day
Double Ninth Day	Lunar New Year	St. Valentine's Day
Easter Day	Parents' Day	White Day
Groundhog Day	Ramadan	Winter Solstice

Discussion Us Groups

- Talk about the questions below.
- Use the Conversation Strategies at the bottom of the page.

1. **Which is your favorite special day?**
   ▶ When is it? What happens on that day? Why do you like it?

2. **What do you know about *Halloween*?**
   ▶ What happens on that day? What does "Trick or Treat" mean?

3. **What do you know about *Saint Patrick's Day*?**
   ▶ What? When? Where? Why? Who? How?

4. **Have you heard of *Martin Luther King Day*?**
   ▶ When is it? What does it celebrate? Why is it important?

5. ***Peace Day, Earth Day*, and *Women's Day* are new special days.**
   ▶ What do you think of these new special days?

6. **Do you know about the '14th' days (February 14, March 14, April 14)?**
   ▶ Tell us about them. What happens on those days?

7. **Are any days celebrated only in your country?**
   ▶ What are they? Talk about them.

8. **What do you think about commercial special days such as *Pepero Day*?**
   ▶ Have special days become too commercial?

9. **Do you think days like Christmas still have their original meaning?**
   ▶ Please explain your opinion.

10. **Do you think that new special days will be made in the future?**
    ▶ What sort of days will they be?

Conversation Strategies

Interrupting:

Excuse me.
Sorry to interrupt.
Can I say something?
Can I make a comment?
Can I add something here?
Do you mind if I say something?
Excuse me for interrupting, but …

Getting back to the topic:

Anyway,
As I was saying,
Where was I?
What was I saying?
We're getting off the topic.
Can we get back to the topic?

Dialogue

- Read this dialogue with your partner.
- Listen to Track 18 on the CD-Rom.
- Perform the dialogue together.
- Change roles. Perform the dialogue again.

Key Words and Expressions

"Guess what?"
"Do you know what I want to tell you?"

fast
go without food

"It says so."
"This information is in this book."

martyrs
people who die for their beliefs

Jenny   Hey, Dad. Guess what?

Dad   I don't know. What is it, Jenny?

Jenny   Have you heard of Ramadan?

Dad   Isn't that when Muslims fast for a month?

Jenny   That's right. They're not allowed to eat anything till the sun goes down. Look. It says so in this book.

Dad   Let me see. Hmm, *Special Days Around the World*.

Jenny   And there's more. Ramadan means extreme heat.

Dad   Interesting. What else did you find out?

Jenny   Well, you know Valentine's Day? In fact it was named after two people, both called Valentine. They were Christian martyrs.

Dad   Don't be silly, Jenny. Everyone knows Valentine's Day is about giving cards, roses and chocolates to your lover.

Jenny   Yes, that's what happens now. But people didn't start giving love letters, or valentines, until the 19th century.

Dad   Amazing.

Jenny   And now it's the second biggest commercial holiday in the world, behind Christmas.

Dad   Really? Can I borrow the book when you've finished with it?

Dialogue Quiz

1. Is Ramadan a national, religious, or commercial festival?
2. When do Muslims eat during Ramadan?
3. Why were the original Valentines killed?
4. How did the modern version of Valentine's Day begin?
5. Do you know any other Saints' Days?
6. Who was St. Swithin? What happens on his day?
7. What is the biggest commercial holiday in the world?

Let's Make a Role-play! Groups

Situation: It is a National Holiday and a couple are staying in a hotel while they visit local tourist attractions. This is the worst hotel they have ever stayed in.

1. Choose your role (Hotel Manager, Receptionist, Mr. Tourist, Mrs. Tourist).
2. Read your role-card and your hints.
3. Think about what you will say in the role-play.
4. Write your ideas on the next page.

Hotel Manager and Receptionist

Here are your hints:

1. Greet the tourists.
2. Ask them what the problem is.
3. Listen carefully to what they say.
4. Apologise.
5. Promise to fix everything.
6. Offer a discount, a refund, or a free dinner.
7. Be polite.

Here are some useful phrases:

- Good morning/afternoon/evening.
- Can I help you?
- I see.
- I understand.
- I'm sorry about that.
- We do apologise.
- Thank you for telling me about this.
- I will get it seen to.
- We will fix it as soon as possible.
- Thank you for your understanding.
- Have a pleasant stay.

Mr. and Mrs. Tourist

Here are your hints:

1. Tell the receptionist you want to make a complaint.
2. Explain that the service in the hotel is terrible.
3. Demand to see the manager.
4. Explain all the problems.
5. Make a final agreement with the manager and the receptionist

Look at pages 36 for some useful conversation strategies. Here are some more that you can use:

We can't sleep because of the discotech.

Please, accept our apologies.

The food is terrible.

The TV doesn't work.

There is no view.

I'm sorry to hear that.

I want to make a complaint.

The bath water is cold.

How can I help you?

There are no towels.

There is no Internet.

My Mind-map

- Fill in the mind-map with your ideas for the role-play.

First of all, ...

Second, ...

Third, ...

Finally, ...

Opinion Samples

- Here are two samples to give you some ideas.

Tourist: I work hard all year and when this National Holiday comes around I want to take a rest and visit local tourist attractions. However, I can't rest in this hotel. The service is terrible. Our room hasn't been cleaned, our window is blocked by a brick wall, there is no hot water, and the food in the morning is inedible. I will be complaining to the travel agent, but now I demand a refund.

Hotel Staff: I do apologize for the inconvenience and I fully understand that you are upset. I really can't imagine how these things have come about. We have been having staff problems lately and it's difficult to find people to work on the National Holiday. I hope you will understand. We will do everything we can to fix the situation. Meanwhile, please accept a free meal tonight in the hotel restaurant, while we fix your room.

Time to Think!

- On Page 35 you made your own special day.
- Now make a poster for your special day and talk about it with your partner.

- Ask each other how you chose your special days.
- Ask what will happen on the special days.
- Talk about your posters together.

5 Role Models

Task 1

- Student A: Think of a famous person (living or dead).
- Other people: Ask questions about the person.
- Student A: Answer "Yes" or "No." Count the questions on the Questions Chart below.
- Other people: Here are some sample questions:

Is this person a man?	Is this person a woman?	Is he/she alive?	Is he/she Korean?
Is he/she American?	Is he/she a sports star?	Is he/she an actor?	Is he/she a pop star?
Is he/she a movie star?	Is he/she on TV?	Is he/she from … ?	Is he/she a writer?
Is he/she a singer?	Is he/she an artist?	Is he/she a poet?	Did he/she …?

Questions Chart

1	2	3	4	5
6	7	8	9	10
11	12	13	14	15
16	17	18	19	20

Task 2

- Interview your partner. Ask these questions and write the answers in the boxes.
- Then change roles and perform the interview again.

Role Model Interview	
Student A: Can I ask you some questions?	**Student B:** Of course. Go ahead.
Who is your favorite movie star?	
Who is your favorite singer?	
Who is your favorite sportsperson?	
Who is your favorite person in history?	
Whom do you admire most?	
Why do you admire him/her?	
What is he/she famous for?	
Do you want to be like him/her?	
Why? Why not?	

Role Models

- Listen to Track 21 on the CD-Rom.
- Read this passage together. who do you think these people are?
- While you read, match the words and phrases at the bottom of the page.
- Then answer the questions on the next page.

 Groups

He is the first Asian to be elected to "the world's most impossible job." Born in Cheongju, in Chungcheongdo province, he graduated from Seoul University. After various government jobs, he worked for South Korea at the United Nations in New York. He says: "I may look soft from the outside, but I have inner strength when it's really necessary."

She was the 2010 Olympic champion, the 2014 silver medalist and three times World Champion. She won a bronze medal at the 2007 World Figure Skating Championships, even though she had back problems. She was born in Gunpo, in Gyeonggido province, and was South Korean national champion six times.

He is 175 cms tall and was famous for his long range free-kick. The first South Korean to play in the British Premier League, he was an attacking, creative midfielder. He helped his country's team get to the World Cup semi-finals in 2002 and played again at the World Cup in Germany in 2006. Although he has retired from football, he is a global club ambassador at Manchester United.

When she was only 11 years old, she won the first prize at the Rostropovich International Cello Competition, in Paris. Since then, she has led the new generation of artists. She performs in the most famous concert halls of Europe, America, and Asia, but also wants to help children to love music: "My task is to make music children's friend."

*The names of these people are in the Answer Key, at the back of the book.

Match the words and phrases on the left to the definitions on the right.

elect	a large region of a country
province	a large stringed instrument of the violin family
graduate	a mix of copper and tin
international	original; imaginative; making possibilities
bronze	over a large distance
bronze medal	the prize for third place
long range	to choose; select
creative	to complete one's studies
cello	worldwide; between nations

There are more reading passages at www.inkbooks.co.kr

Comprehension Check

1. What do the four people on page 42 have in common?
2. What is 'the world's most impossible job'?
3. Who was well-known for his long free-kicks?
4. Who won a medal despite her back problems?
5. Who won a first prize before she was a teenager?
6. What does 'new generation of artists' mean?
7. Can you explain 'creative midfielder'?
8. Ban Gi-moon is 175 cms tall. ☐ True ☐ False ☐ Not in the passage.
9. Hanna Jang became World Junior Champion in 2006. ☐ True ☐ False
10. Park Ji-sung played in two World Cup Competitions. ☐ True ☐ False
11. Kim Yu-na won third prize at the 2007 WFS Championships. ☐ True ☐ False

Think for Yourself

☐ Whom do you admire?
☐ What values would you like to have?
☐ What lifestyle would you like to have?

Qualities of Role Models

With your partner: Look at these Role-Model qualities.

- Which do you think is most important?
- Which do you think is least important?
- Number the qualities from 1 to 15.

___ honest	___ wealthy	___ happy
___ diligent	___ strong	___ powerful
___ successful	___ humble	___ intelligent
___ good-looking	___ sincere	___ funny
___ generous	___ confident	___ creative

Choose three qualities for yourself:

1. _____ 2. _____ 3. _____

Discussion Us Groups

- Talk about the questions below.
- Use the Conversation Strategies at the bottom of the page.

1 Talk about your role model.
  ▶ Lifestyle, personality, occupation, etc.

2 Do you want to be successful?
  ▶ Why? Why not? Support your opinion.

3 What are the advantages and disadvantages of being famous?

4 Would you like to interview a famous person?
  ▶ What questions would you ask?

5 "The best teachers are the lives of great men and women."
  ▶ What does this statement mean?
  ▶ Do you agree? Why? Why not?

6 "Rather than money or fame, give me truth."
  ▶ What does this statement mean?
  ▶ Do you agree? Why? Why not?

7 Have you heard of The American Dream?
  ▶ Explain it to the other group members.
  ▶ Talk about your dream.

8 Imagine that you are a role model for other people.
  ▶ Which of your qualities do you want other people to copy?
  ▶ Which qualities do you not want people to copy?

Conversation Strategies

Adding comments	Expressing opinions
By the way,	I think ….
Incidentally,	I suppose …
In addition,	I feel that …
Furthermore,	I believe …
Speaking of ….	In my opinion,
I forgot to say that …	As I see it,
That reminds me.	It seems to me …
While we're on the subject, …	As far as I can tell,

Dialogue

- Listen to Track 22 on the CD-Rom.
- Read the dialogue with your partners.
- Perform the dialogue together.
- Change roles. Perform the dialogue again.

Seung-min	Hello, Mrs. Brown. Have you seen Kevin?
Grandma	No, I haven't, Seung-min. What's up?
Seung-min	I want to ask him about this homework.
Grandma	Maybe I can help. What's the problem?
Seung-min	I can't figure it out. What's the difference between a role model and a hero?
Grandma	That's a tricky one. I suppose heroes can be role models, but not every role model is a hero.
Seung-min	What? I still don't get it.
Grandma	OK. Think of someone you really admire, like a doctor or …
Seung-min	Or an artist?
Grandma	That's right. Well, not every artist is a hero, saving lives and fighting for his country.
Seung-min	Ah. I think I see what you mean.
Grandma	But an artist can be a role model if you want to follow his example.
Seung-min	I'm with you now. Ah! Here's Kevin.
Kevin	Hey, Seung-min. Have you figured out the homework?
Seung-min	No sweat, Kevin. It's a piece of cake. Let me explain …

Key Words and Expressions

"What's up?"
"What's the matter?"
"What's the problem?"

figure it out
understand, find the answer

tricky
difficult; not simple

"I don't get it."
"I don't understand."

"I'm with you."
"I understand."

"No sweat."
"No problem."

Dialogue Quiz

1. Why is Seung-min looking for Kevin?
2. What is Seung-min's problem?
3. Does Seung-min want to be a hero?
4. Does Kevin want to be an artist?
5. Do you agree with Grandma's explanation?
6. Write the names of three Korean heroes below. Are they role models as well as heroes?

1. _____   2. _____   3. _____

Let's Debate

- In this Unit we will begin to debate.
- Debating is a more formal way of discussing.
- Debating uses conversation strategies and role-play strategies.
- First, let's play a debating game. Here are the rules:

Just a Minute!

Speaker 1: Talk about your role model for one minute.
Everyone else: When Speaker 1 pauses, say "Hesitation!"
When Speaker 1 goes off the topic, say "Deviation!"
When Speaker 1 repeats something, say "Repetition!"
Speaker 2: Talk about your role model for one minute.
[Continue until everyone has talked for one minute.]

- Here are some famous debaters.
- Do you know who they are?
- What do you know about them?

Famous debaters who became leaders

O.W. competed in Debates in high school and at the National Forenslcs League nationals.

G.W.B. was on Yale University's debate team.

M.T. debated politics and economics at Oxford University.

M.G. was famous for debating politics, religion and culture.

N.M. saw debate as part of the democratic process.

A.L. was a great American debater and orator.

The full names are in the back of the book, in the Answer Section.

Debate Corner Us Groups

1 In your group, choose one of the statements (motions) below.

- Everyone needs a role-model.
- Parents are the best role models.
- Success comes from working hard.
- Love is more important than money.

2 Choose one pair of people (Pro) to agree with your motion.

3 The other pair (Con) will disagree with the motion.
☐ Pro pair: Write three reasons for agreeing with the motion, plus your conclusion.
☐ Con pair: Write three reasons for disagreeing with the motion, plus your conclusion.

First of all, ...

Next, ...

Furthermore, ...

In conclusion, ...

4 Use these disagreeing phrases when you debate (next page).

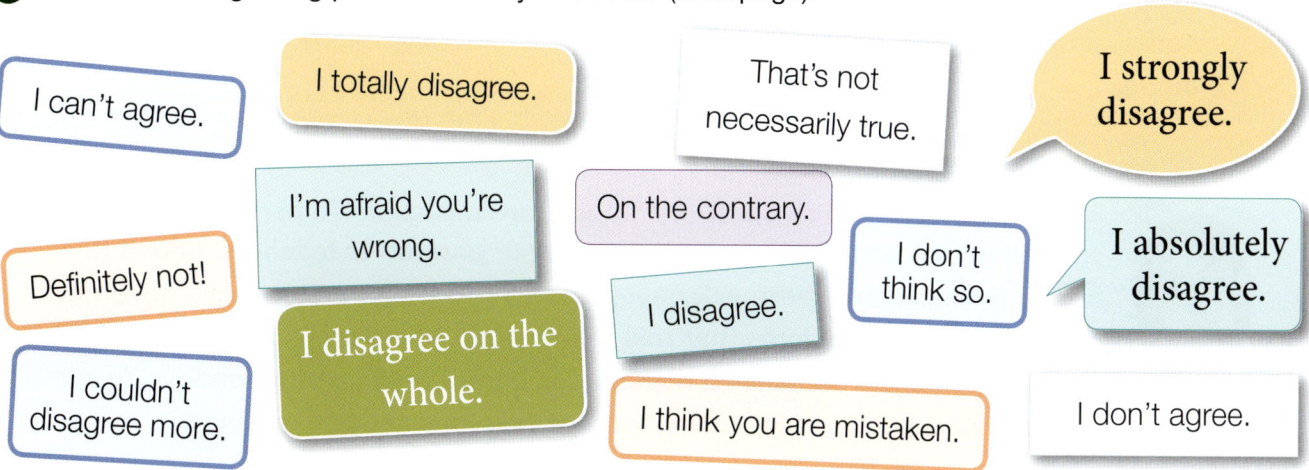

I can't agree.
I totally disagree.
That's not necessarily true.
I strongly disagree.
I'm afraid you're wrong.
On the contrary.
I don't think so.
I absolutely disagree.
Definitely not!
I disagree.
I disagree on the whole.
I couldn't disagree more.
I think you are mistaken.
I don't agree.

Unit 5 Special Days 47

Let's Debate! Us Groups

1. Pro Pair, Student 1: Explain your three reasons.
2. Con Pair, Student 1: Explain your three reasons.
3. Pro Pair, Student 2: Disagree with the Con Pair and give your conclusion.
   Use the phrases on page 47.
4. Con Pair, Student 2: Disagree with the Pro Pair and give your conclusion.
   Use the phrases on page 47.

- Here is a sample debate on the topic "Everyone needs a role-model."

Pro Speaker 1: First of all, let me say that my partner and I agree with the motion. We believe that everyone needs a role model. I will give you three reasons. First, role models give us guidance when we are young. We can learn by copying them. Second, they help us with self-improvement. Third, They give us good examples.

 **Con Speaker 1:** My partner and I will show you why we don't need role-models. To start with, role models are not always good people. The role models we see in movies are often too violent. Next, role models are just human. They don't always give us a good example. Furthermore, we can't live our own lives if we are copying other people.

Pro Speaker 2: I disagree with Con Speaker 1. He is very wrong. Let me tell you why. First, role models such as parents or teachers help us to make decisions. Second, they have often had the same problems and they can show us how to solve them. Third, it is not necessarily true that all movie role models are violent. Some of them are very good people. In conclusion, I think we should pass the motion that everyone needs a role model.

 **Con Speaker 2:** Pro Speakers 1 and 2 are mistaken. To begin with they are saying that we have to be the same as our parents or teachers. I don't think so. If we do this there will never be any progress. Second, we have new and different problems that role models can't help us to solve. Third, self-improvement is personal. It doesn't come from copying other people. To sum up, I hope we will reject the motion that everyone needs a role model.

6 Family

Brainstorming

- How many people are there in your family?
- What are their names?

Task 1
- Look at this Family Word Search.
- Can you find all these words?

aunt	family	husband	sister
brother	father	mother	son
cousin	grandfather	niece	uncle
daughter	grandmother	nephew	wife

*The solution is in the Answer Key, at the back of the book.

					X							
				N	O	G						
			C	I	V	R	L					
			H	U	S	B	A	N	D			
		E	Z	H	U	U	N	C	L	E		
R	E	H	T	O	M	D	N	A	R	G		
E	T	G	N	C	E	F	I	W	E	S		
H			H	E	A	A			T	I		
T			N	M	P	T			H	S		
O	P	O	I			H	N	K	G	T		
R	S	L	E			E	E	U	U	E		
B	Y	Z	C			R	W	W	A	R		
Q	C	F	E			Y	O	Z	D	X		

Task 2
- Make your family tree. Write the names of all your family members.
- Explain your family tree to someone else.

My _____'s name:

My _____'s name:

My _____'s name:

My _____'s name:

My _____'s name:

My _____'s name:

My _____'s name:

My _____'s name:

My _____'s name:

The Korean Family

- Listen to Track 23 on the CD-Rom.
- Read this passage together.
- While you read, match the words and phrases at the bottom of the page.
- Then answer the questions on the next page.

The Korean family has changed greatly in recent years. Sixty years ago, it was normal for three generations to share the same house. Now, however, this is very rare. Fifty-five percent of families consist of only one or two generations and the number of children in these nuclear families is constantly falling. In fact, the size of the average household in 2014 was only 2.7 people, compared with 4.5 in 1980, and 5.5 in 1966.

This change has happened for a number of reasons. First, Korean culture was damaged by the Japanese occupation (1910–45) and the Korean War (1950–53). Then, from the 1960s, Korea changed from a farming society to an industrialized society, quickly taking on western values and technology. As a result, the traditional extended family has given way to the modern nuclear family, and the number of divorces and single mothers is increasing.

Attitudes are also changing. Many young people these days do not want to live with their parents and look after them in old age, though this used to be their duty. They feel that elderly parents should stay in nursing homes, or that society should take care of them. Even the parents feel bad about depending on their children for support.

As with many developed countries, the changing family in Korea is producing an aging population, with fewer young people to take care of the economy. This situation is a major problem for everyone.

Match the words and phrases on the left to the definitions on the right.

nuclear family	a woman who looks after her children by herself
household	an institute for looking after old and sick people
damaged	harmed; hurt; injured
extended family	relying on
divorce	parents and children living together
single mother	people are living longer
attitude	people living in a house
nursing home	the ending of a marriage
depending on	three (or more) generations living together
aging population	way of thinking

50 Active English Discussion 1

There are more reading passages at www.inkbooks.co.kr

Comprehension Check

1. What does 'three generations' in lines 1 and 2 of the passage mean?
2. How many generations make up a nuclear family?
3. How big was the average household in 1980?
4. Why has the extended family given way to the nuclear family?
5. Do all young people want to take care of their parents?
6. What do they think should happen to elderly parents?
7. Why is this situation a big problem?

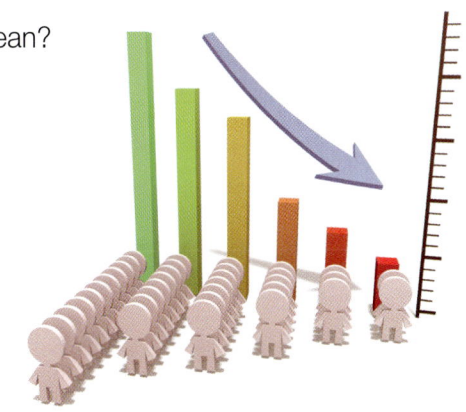

Think for Yourself

- ☐ Do you want to take care of your parents when they get old?
- ☐ Do you want to have your own family and children?
- ☐ Who will look after you when you are elderly?

Background Information

Did you know?

- ☐ Korea's birthrate (8.6 babies per 1000 citizens) is one of the lowest in the world.
- ☐ Korean parents with one child spend 23.8 % of their income on education. Those with two children spend 59 %, and those with three children spend 63.9 %.
- ☐ There are about 250 Korean family names.
- ☐ 45 % of Korean people are called Kim, Lee, or Park.
- ☐ Filial piety ('hyo' in Korean) was traditionally at the heart of Korean family life.
- ☐ In English, 'uncle' can mean 'my father's brother' or 'my mother's brother.' In Korea, these relatives have different titles.
- ☐ Members of the same generation in a Korean family often have the same generation name. For example: Kim Sung-min, Kim Sung-jun.
- ☐ Since the 1970s, parents started giving their children names based on Korean words, instead of Chinese characters.

Discussion Groups

- Talk together about the questions below.
- Use the Conversation Strategies at the bottom of the page.

1. **Do you prefer the extended family or the nuclear family?**
   ▶ Explain your opinion.

2. **Is it better to be a single child or to have brothers and sisters?**
   ▶ Explain you opinion.

3. **What are 'family values'?**
   ▶ Why are they important?

4. **What is 'character education'?**
   ▶ Who should teach this to children? Parents or school teachers?
   ▶ Clarify your opinion.

5. **What does this picture tell us about Korean families?**
   ▶ Hint: Grandparent, child, dog

6. **What do you think about the falling birthrate?**
   ▶ What effect will it have on jobs?
   ▶ What effect will it have on the economy?
   ▶ How will it affect elderly people?

7. **Why are fewer couples having children these days?**
   ▶ Support your opinion.

8. **Why is the number of divorces and single mothers increasing?**
   ▶ What do you think about this situation?

9. **Many farmers are marrying foreign wives these days.**
   ▶ Why is this?
   ▶ What effect will it have on Korean society?

Conversation Strategies

Restating someone's opinion:

In other words,
Let me get this right.
So you mean that …
So you're saying that …
What you're saying is that …
If I understand you correctly,

"… the average number of children in a family is now less than 2."

Confirming your opinion:

Yes, I suppose so.
You could say that.
That's it.
Yes, you've got it.
That's right.
Absolutely.

Dialogue

- Listen to Track 24 on the CD-Rom.
- Read the dialogue with your partner.
- Perform the dialogue together.
- Change roles. Perform the dialogue again.

Key Words and Expressions

"Things were different then."
"Life was different then, so people acted differently."

"We'll see."
"Let's wait and see what happens. You might change your mind."

Grandma Brown	Hello Kevin. What's up?
Kevin	Hi, Grandma. Can I ask you a question?
Grandma Brown	Sure. What is it?
Kevin	I hope it's not too personal.
Grandma Brown	You won't find out if you don't ask.
Kevin	Well, … how many children did your parents have?
Grandma Brown	Let me see. I had three brothers and two sisters.
Kevin	Wow! That's a lot.
Grandma Brown	Oh yes. Things were different then.
Kevin	What do you mean?
Grandma Brown	In my parents' day, it was normal to have a large number of children. The mother used to stay home and look after them.
Kevin	I've heard about that.
Grandma Brown	There days, married couples both want a job, so they don't have many children. Some don't have any.
Kevin	Why do they get married, then?
Grandma Brown	Perhaps they just like living together, Kevin.
Kevin	I suppose so.
Grandma Brown	Let's talk about it again when you get married.
Kevin	Don't worry. That won't happen.
Grandma Brown	We'll see, Kevin. We'll see.

Dialogue Quiz

1. How many children did Grandma Brown's parents have?
2. Was this number of children unusual?
3. What was the mother's role in those days?
4. Has this role changed?
5. Does Kevin want to get married?
6. Does Grandma Brown think that he will get married?

Let's Debate Groups

❶ This is our second debate. It is about the family.
❷ When we debate, our arguments should be factual.
❸ So, let's think about the difference between facts and opinions.
❹ Identify the facts (F) and opinions (O) in the following statements. If you think the statement could be a fact or an opinion, check "NS" (Not sure).

	Fact or Opinion?	F	O	NS
1	London is the capital of England.			
2	London is the best city to visit in Europe.			
3	Spring is the best season to visit London.			
4	Buckingham Palace is in London.			
5	Arsenal Football Club is in London.			
6	Football is better than baseball.			
7	Swimming is good for health.			
8	Healthy body, healthy mind.			
9	Smoking is an unhealthy habit.			
10	Secondhand smoke harms children.			
11	An apple a day keeps the doctor away.			
12	Family values are important.			
13	Honesty is the quality of being truthful.			
14	Honesty is the best policy.			
15	Parents should not punish their children.			
16	Money can't buy happiness.			
17	Nature is more important than nurture.			
18	Like father like son.			

The answers are in the back of the book, in the Answer Section.

- When you present your arguments (next page), use facts and examples.
- When the other side speaks, look out for opinion-based arguments.

Debate Corner Us Groups

1 In your group, choose one of the propositions below.

- Family values are disappearing.
- Children should take care of their elderly parents.
- Having children is too expensive these days.
- Nature is more important than nurture in character education.

2 Choose one pair of people (Pro) to agree with your proposition.

3 The other pair (Con) will disagree with the proposition.
- ☐ Pro pair: Write three reasons for agreeing with the proposition, plus your conclusion.
- ☐ Con pair: Write three reasons for disagreeing with the proposition, plus your conclusion.

First of all, ...
_____
_____
_____

Next, ...
_____
_____
_____

Furthermore, ...
_____
_____
_____

In conclusion, ...
_____
_____
_____

Let's Begin!

1 Pro Pair, Student 1: Explain your three reasons.
2 Con Pair, Student 1: Explain your three reasons.
3 Pro Pair, Student 2: Disagree with the Con Pair and give your conclusion.
   Use the phrases at the bottom of the page.
4 Con Pair, Student 2: Disagree with the Pro Pair and give your conclusion.
   Use the phrases at the bottom of the page.

- That's not necessarily true.
- Definitely not!
- I'm afraid you're wrong.
- I don't think so.
- I think you are mistaken.
- On the contrary.
- I can't agree.
- I disagree.

Unit 6 Family 55

Argument Samples

- Here are two samples to give you some ideas (Tracks 25 and 26).
- They are about the proposition "Family values are disappearing".
- Can you identify the facts and opinions in these samples?

Pro Speaker 1: I am in favor of the proposition. In my opinion family values are disappearing these days. In the traditional extended family, three or more generations lived together, and it was the duty of the oldest son to take care of his parents and grandparents. However, young people these days prefer to live by themselves and send their parents to nursing homes. The nuclear family is not only destroying our traditional values but it is also causing divorces and single mothers.

Con Speaker 1: I am against the proposition. Korea is a developed country now, and just as in other developed countries, young people don't want to be burdened with elderly parents or lots of children. The extended family is not relevant any more in our high technology society. Looking after a child is becoming more and more expensive and time-consuming, and young wives want to have their own careers. This is a time of opportunity and equality.

Reflection

- Let's do a self-assessment about your study methods.
- Efficient study methods lead to effective discussion skills.
- 5 = Always, 4 = Usually, 3 = Sometimes, 2 = Seldom, 1 = Never.

	My Study Methods	1	2	3	4	5
1	I look at today's Unit before coming to class.					
2	I check the vocabulary in the Unit before class.					
3	I look at the online activities for the Unit by myself.					
4	In class I do my best in everything.					
5	I work well with my group members.					
6	I give ideas to my group members.					
7	I ask the teacher if I need help.					
8	After class I look at the Unit again.					
9	Then I prepare for the next Unit.					

- What is your score out of 45?
- How can you improve your study methods?

7 School Life

Task 1
- Think of a typical school day. What do you do each day?
- Ask your partner about the actions in the table below: "What time do you …?"

do homework	get up	brush your teeth	have a break	play with friends
eat dinner	go home	go to school	have breakfast	wash your face
get dressed	go to bed	go to sleep	have lunch	watch TV

Task 2

Survey
- Choose four things from the table and write them below (A, B, C, D).
- Then ask your questions to five people (1, 2, 3, 4, 5).
- Write their answers in the boxes.

A. What time do you _____?

1. _____ 2. _____ 3. _____ 4. _____ 5. _____

B. What time do you _____?

1. _____ 2. _____ 3. _____ 4. _____ 5. _____

C. What time do you _____?

1. _____ 2. _____ 3. _____ 4. _____ 5. _____

D. What time do you _____?

1. _____ 2. _____ 3. _____ 4. _____ 5. _____

Task 3

Diary
- Write about your typical school day:

I wake up at _____ a.m. Then I brush my teeth and wash my face.

Next, I _____

At _____

At _____

At _____

At _____

Unit 7 School Life 57

Learning by Doing

- Listen to Track 27 on the CD-Rom.
- Read this passage together.
- While you read, match the words and phrases at the bottom of the page.
- Then answer the questions on the next page.

 Groups

Children in this school start the day by saying hello to all the staff. It's normal to call the teachers by their first names, since everyone wants school to be a pleasant and exciting place. In the classrooms, pupils choose their weekly goals with their teachers and then carry out tasks at their own pace.

Teaching is practical, encouraging students to do things by themselves. Instead of simply memorizing information, children walk around, collect information, ask the teacher for advice, and cooperate with other pupils. Even in language lessons, teachers use role plays, songs, games, videos, and dramas. There are no discipline problems, since the teacher is always in control.

This isn't a special school. It's a normal comprehensive school in Finland. Even though they have such a student-friendly, stress-free approach to learning, the 2012 PISA* survey of 65 countries showed that Finnish teenagers scored just below their Korean counterparts in math and reading, and above them in science. These results are due to a number of factors. First of all, Finnish teachers are highly qualified. Secondly, pupils have only one teacher between the ages of 9 and 16. Thirdly, students learn by doing, and develop higher-order thinking skills.

Finland has a similar economic history to Korea and their languages share similar roots. Could the Finnish education system be used in Korea? It's certainly food for thought!

*Programme for International Student Assessment

Match the words and phrases on the left to the definitions on the right.

staff	active, critical, logical thinking
at their own pace	all together; whole; multi-level
cooperate	at their own speed
role plays	bad behavior; loss of control
discipline problems	between the ages of 13 and 19
comprehensive	expert; professional
teenager	people who work in the school
counterpart	reason; cause
factor	small dramas; real-life situations
highly qualified	someone with the same role
high-order thinking	something to think about
food for thought	work together

There are more reading passages at www.inkbooks.co.kr

Comprehension Check

1. How does a typical school day start in Finland?
2. Who chooses the learning goals for the week?
3. Do students all learn the same things?
4. Do students sit at their desks all day?
5. Do students have to remember lots of information?
6. Can you find another word for 'students' in the reading passage?
7. Give one reason for the success of Finnish education.

Think for Yourself

- How does the day start in your school?
- Do you know your teacher's first name?
- Is your school a pleasant and exciting place?
- Would you like to have the same teacher for seven years?
- If you were Minister of Education, what would you change?

Background Information

Did you know?

- Children in Australia go to school for an average of 16.2 years.
- Children in Chad (Africa) go to school for an average of 3.9 years.
- Education in New Zealand is free between the ages of 6 and 15.
- Every day, 3,000 students drop out of school in the USA. Their lives are on average 9.2 years shorter than the lives of high school graduates.
- In Nepal, students have two months holiday during the monsoon. The school week is from Sunday to Friday morning.
- Over 115 million children of elementary school age around the world do not go to school. Nearly 60% of these are girls.
- Over 860 million people in the world cannot read. 61% come from Bangladesh, China, India and Pakistan. 66% are women.
- According to the UN, education reduces poverty, improves general health, and stops the spread of HIV and AIDS.

Discussion Groups

- Discuss the questions below.
- Use the Conversation Strategies at the bottom of the page.

1. **What is your favorite school subject?**
   ▸ Why do you like it?

2. **Who is your favorite teacher?**
   ▸ Why do you like him / her?

3. **Is there a subject you want to learn that is not taught at school?**
   ▸ What is it? Please explain.

4. **Do you do an extra-curricular activity? (Choir, Drama club, Chess club, etc.)**
   ▸ Yes? Tell everyone about it.
   ▸ No? Why not?

5. **Do you agree with school uniforms?**
   ▸ Why do you agree/disagree?

6. **What is the purpose of education?**
   ▸ Why do we go to school?

7. **Should everyone learn the same subjects at school?**
   ▸ Should we be able to choose our favorite subjects?
   ▸ Why are Math and English important?
   ▸ What about artistic subjects (Music, Art, Drama, Dance, Craftwork, etc.)?

8. **Imagine that you are the Minister of Education.**
   ▸ How will you change the education system?

9. **What is home schooling? Do you agree with it?**
   ▸ Why? Why not? Support your opinion.

Conversation Strategies

Giving Information:

To start with,
To begin with,
First of all,
Next,
Finally,

Adding Information:

Also,
Besides,
Furthermore,
In addition,
And another thing,

Dialogue

- Listen to Track 28 on the CD-Rom.
- Read this dialogue with your partner.
- Perform the dialogue together.
- Change roles. Perform the dialogue again.

(Kevin is sitting on the sofa, watching TV. Mr. Brown enters the room.)

Dad   What are you doing, Kevin?

Kevin   Hi, Dad. I'm watching reality TV. It's great.

Dad   Don't you think you should be doing your homework?

Kevin   I don't want to, Dad. It's too boring.

Dad   We can't always do what we like, you know.

Kevin   Give me a break, Dad. I just want to take it easy and relax.

Dad   I understand, Kevin. But the fact is …

Kevin   I know, I know. I've heard it all before, Dad.

Dad   We only want the best for you, Kevin.

Kevin   Sorry, Dad. I know you mean well. But …

Dad   But what?

Kevin   Well, it's easy for you. You don't have all these subjects to study.

Dad   C'mon, Kevin. Don't put off till tomorrow what you can do today.

Kevin   I suppose you're right. Oh, well. I'd better do my homework.

Key Words and Expressions

reality TV
television shows in which people are put in 'real life' situations

"Give me a break."
"Please understand me."

take it easy
have a rest; relax

"I've hear it all before."
"We've talked about this many times." "I know what you're going to say."

"You mean well."
"Your intentions are good." "I know you're trying to help."

Dialogue Quiz

1. Why isn't Kevin doing his homework?
2. What is he doing instead?
3. Do you think his father is angry?
4. Does his father want to help Kevin?
5. What does "Don't put off till tomorrow what you can do today" mean?
6. What do you think of reality TV?

Debate Corner

In your group, choose one of the propositions below.

- Your school years are the best years of your life.
- Physical education and nutrition are more important school subjects than math and English.
- Teachers should get more pay than doctors.
- School uniforms should be banned.

2. Choose one pair (Pro) to agree with your proposition, one pair (Con) to disagree with it, and (if there are 5 people in your group) one person to be the Timekeeper.

Pro/Con Pair, Speaker 1:
▶ These phrases will help you present your arguments.

First of all …	The main thing is …	Furthermore …
To begin with …	The most important thing is …	What's more, …
For a start …	Most importantly …	I might add that …
Next, …	We have to consider that	Not to mention that …
In addition, …	On the one hand …	Plus the fact that …
Finally, …	On the other hand …	Not only that, but …

Pro/Con Pair, Speaker 2
▶ These phrases will help you to reject the other team's arguments.

I disagree.	That isn't the point.	You are mistaken.
I disagree entirely.	That's debatable.	I'm not sure about that.
On the contrary.	That's very unlikely.	I don't know about that.
Definitely not!	That isn't strictly true.	That depends …
That's ridiculous!	I'm afraid you're wrong.	That's a good point, but …
You can't be serious!	I'm afraid I can't agree.	You have a point, but …

Timekeeper: These phrases will help you control the debate.

Today's proposition is …	Speaking for the proposition is ….
You have two minutes to speak.	Speaking against the proposition is ….
Your time is up.	The next speaker is …
Next speaker please.	The proposition has been accepted.
Your conclusions please.	The proposition has been rejected.

Let's Debate!

1. **Pro Pair:** Write three reasons for agreeing with the proposition, plus your conclusion.
2. **Con Pair:** Write three reasons for disagreeing with the proposition, plus your conclusion.
3. **Timekeeper:** Look at pages 62 and 64 and think of how to start and end the debate.

First of all, ...
_____
_____
_____

Next, ...
_____
_____
_____

Furthermore, ...
_____
_____
_____

In conclusion, ...
_____
_____
_____

There are some sample arguments on the next page.

Let's Begin!

Timekeeper:

1. Start the debate (see pages 62 and 64).

2. Ask the first Pro speaker to state the 'Pro' arguments.
   Tell him/her that he/she has 2 minutes.

3. Ask the first Con speaker to state the 'Con' arguments.
   Tell him/her that he/she has 2 minutes.

4. Ask the second Pro student to speak and give his/her conclusions.
   Tell him/her that he/she has 2 minutes.

5. Ask the second Con student to speak and give his/her conclusions.
   Tell him/her that he/she has 2 minutes.

6. End the debate (see pages 62 and 64). Either you can decide which team had the best arguments, or you can ask another group to decide.

Debate Sample

- Here is a sample to give you some ideas (Track 29).
- The proposition is "School uniforms should be banned."
- Can you find the phrases from pages 55 and 62?

Timekeeper: Today's debate is on the proposition "School uniforms should be banned." Speaker one for the Pro Team, please give your arguments in favor of the proposition. You have two minutes.

Pro Speaker 1: I am in favor of the proposition. To begin with, school uniforms destroy personal identity. Students become one of a crowd, looking the same as everyone else. Secondly, they prevent students from learning how to choose their clothes well. They cannot be creative with their clothes. Most importantly, uniforms can be very expensive. Students have to buy at least two full sets of summer and winter uniforms, plus physical education outfits.

Timekeeper: Thank you. Now I call upon Speaker one for the Con Team. Please give your rebuttal of Pro Speaker 1's arguments. You have two minutes.

Con Speaker 1: I disagree entirely with Pro Speaker 1. I am afraid he is mistaken. For a start, school uniforms do not destroy identity. On the contrary, they make students proud of being part of a team. As for clothes sense, that's a good point, but without uniforms, wealthy children can wear expensive clothes and laugh at those wearing old, cheap clothes. Finally, I can't agree about the cost. Uniforms can last for a long time and don't have to be replaced according to fashion.

Timekeeper: Thank you. Now I call upon the audience. You have heard the arguments for and against the proposition that school uniforms should be banned. All in favor of the proposition, please raise your hands. All those against the proposition, please raise your hands. I now declare that the proposition has been accepted/rejected.

Further Reading: There are more debate links and interesting activities at www.inkbooks.co.kr.

Unit 8 Sport

Brainstorming

- Are you a sports player or a sports watcher?
- Which sports do you like (✔) and which do you dislike (✗)?

archery ☐	badminton ☐	baseball ☐	basketball ☐	cycling ☐
football ☐	golf ☐	ice-hockey ☐	running ☐	skating ☐
soccer ☐	swimming ☐	table-tennis ☐	tennis ☐	volleyball ☐

Task 1

- You are going to take a survey of people in the class.
- Write the names of different sports in the boxes below.
- Ask your 4 questions to everybody in the class: "Do you prefer _____ to _____?"
- Count the number of "Yes" answers and "No" answers.

1. Do you prefer _____ to _____ ? ☐ Yes ☐ No
2. Do you prefer _____ to _____ ? ☐ Yes ☐ No
3. Do you prefer _____ to _____ ? ☐ Yes ☐ No
4. Do you prefer _____ to _____ ? ☐ Yes ☐ No

Task 2

- Summarize your results.
- For example: "On the whole, people prefer swimming to golf."

On the whole, ...

In general, ...

Overall, ...

By and large, ...

All in all, ...

The Olympic Spirit

- Listen to Track 30 on the CD-Rom.
- Read this passage together.
- While you read, match the words and phrases at the bottom of the page.
- Then answer the questions on the next page.

The Olympic Games go back to 776 BC, and were held on the plains of Olympia, in Greece. They were banned in 393 AD, and didn't start again until 1500 years later. In 1894, the Frenchman, Pierre de Coubertin, created the International Olympic Committee (IOC), and the 1st modern Olympic Games were held in Athens on April 6, 1896.

Promoting peace has always been an important part of the Olympic spirit. In times of war, a truce was made between the fighting armies, so that people could travel safely to the Games. This 'Olympic Truce' could be seen in the 2000 and 2004 Summer Olympics and the 2006 Winter Olympics, when North and South Korea marched under the same flag.

The goal of the original Games was to balance body and mind, in a spirit of peace, friendship and fair play. For the original Olympian athletes, taking part was more important than winning. Modern athletes, on the other hand, are under a lot of pressure to win gold medals for their countries.

rmnoa357 / Shutterstock.com

A recent addition to the Olympics is the Paralympics, in which handicapped people take part in 12 sports. The International Paralympic Committee (IPC) began in 1989 and is a non-profit organization. It aims to develop sporting opportunities for disabled people and promotes values such as courage, determination, motivation, and equality.

Match the words and phrases on the left to the definitions on the right.

go back to 776	a time when armies agree not to fight
banned	assist; encourage; work for
truce	balance; sameness
fair play	desire; wish
athlete	drive; energy; diligence
handicapped people	evenness; equal treatment
non-profit	people with damaged bodies or minds
promote	player; sportsperson
determination	started in 776
motivation	stopped; finished
equality	using all its money to run the organization

Comprehension Check

1. What does 'IOC' mean?
2. What does 'IPC' mean?
3. What are the goals of the Olympic Games?
4. What are the goals of the Paralympics?
5. How long did the original Olympics continue?
6. Did the Modern Olympics start in France?
7. How are modern athletes different from the original athletes?
8. What does 'Olympic Truce' mean?
9. Can you find another word for 'handicapped' in the passage?

Zhao jian kang / Shutterstock.com

Think for Yourself

- [ ] Where were the 2000 and 2004 Summer Olympics held?
- [ ] Where were the 2008, 2012 and 2016 Summer Olympics held?
- [ ] Where were the 2006, 2010 and 2014 Winter Olympics held?
- [ ] What does the Olympic logo mean?
- [ ] Why were the games banned in 393 AD?
- [ ] Are the original Olympic ideas followed today?

Background Information

Did you know?

- [ ] The Olympic motto is "Citius, Altius, Fortius" ("Swifter, Higher, Stronger").
- [ ] The Olympic flame is lit in Olympia by women wearing greek robes. They use a curved mirror and the sun to light the flame.
- [ ] The Olympic Torch is carried by many different runners from Olympia to the hosting city.
- [ ] The last Olympic gold medals made entirely out of gold were awarded in 1912.
- [ ] The first Winter Olympics were held in 1924 in Chamonix, France .
- [ ] 204 countries participated in the 2012 Summer Olympics in London.
- [ ] Only four athletes have won medals at both the Winter and Summer Olympic Games.
- [ ] The youngest athlete to win a medal was Dimities Loundras, in 1896. He was 10 years and 218 days old.
- [ ] The oldest person to win a medal was Oscar Swahn, who was 72 when he won a silver medal in the Antwerp Games of 1920.
- [ ] London is the only city to host the Olympics three times: 1908, 1948 and 2012.

Unit 8 Sport

Discussion Us Groups

- Talk together about the questions below.
- Use the Conversation Strategies at the bottom of the page.

1. **What's your favorite sport?**
   - Tell us about it.

2. **Do you have a role model who is a sports star?**
   - Tell us about him or her.
   - Why do sports stars become fashion idols?

3. **Do you like to watch sports on TV?**
   - Why? Why not? Support your opinion.

4. **Do you ever watch sports live at a stadium?**
   - Why? Why not? Support your opinion.

5. **Do you like to play sports?**
   - Why? Why not? Support your opinion.

6. **Do you think professional sports people get too much money?**
   - Explain your opinion.

7. **Is the original Olympic spirit still alive?**
   - Are the Olympics too commercial?
   - Is there too much drug-taking?
   - Is there too much nationalism?

8. **The UCLA Bruins football coach, "Red" Sanders, said in 1950 "Men, I'll be honest. Winning isn't everything." Then he paused and said "Men, it's the only thing!" What do you think? Is sport all about winning?**

Conversation Strategies

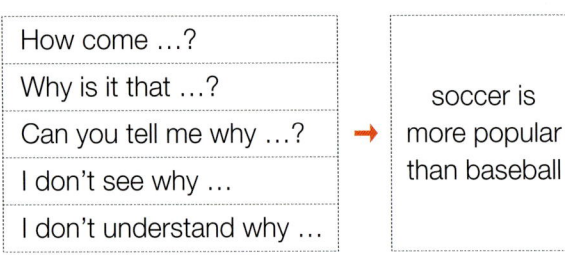

Asking for explanation:

How come …?
Why is it that …?
Can you tell me why …?
I don't see why …
I don't understand why …

→ soccer is more popular than baseball

Responding :

Maybe it's because …	→	Korean soccer stars are so famous
It could be that …		

I'm not sure.	Me either.
I don't know.	I have no idea.
Search me.	You tell me.

Dialogue

- Listen to Track 31 on the CD-Rom.
- Read this dialogue with your partners. Perform the dialogue together.
- Change roles. Perform the dialogue again.

(Kevin and Seung-min are sitting on the sofa, watching TV. Mr. Brown enters the room.)

Mr. Brown	Hello, you two couch potatoes.
Kevin	Hello, dad.
Mr. Brown	Haven't you got anything better to do today?
Seung-min	But, Mr. Brown, it's the Rose Bowl.
Mr. Brown	I see. That's different. Who's playing?
Seung-min	It's Michigan against Stanford University.
Kevin	Yes. It's really exciting, dad.
Mr. Brown	Did you say Michigan and Stanford?
Seung-min	Yes. Why do you ask?
Mr. Brown	Believe it or not, the first Rose Bowl game, in 1902, was between the same two teams.
Kevin	Wow. That's a coincidence!
Seung-min	1902. That's more than 100 years ago.
Mr. Brown	That's right. You can see why the Rose Bowl is called The Granddaddy of them all.
Kevin	*(Looking out of the window)* Why is mum waving at you, dad?
Mr. Brown	Oh, I forgot. I promised to take her skating. Let me know who wins.
Kevin	OK, dad. See you later.

Key Words and Expressions

"Haven't you got anything better to do today?"
"Why are you being lazy?"
"Don't you have any work or other things to do?"

"That's different."
"I understand."
"That's a special case."

coincidence
accident; chance; two things happening at the same time

Dialogue Quiz

1. What is the date today? (Check the date of the Rose Bowl.)
2. Why does Mr. Brown call Kevin and Seung-min couch potatoes?
3. What does 'them all' mean in 'The Granddaddy of them all'?
4. Does Mr. Brown watch the game with the two boys?
5. How will Mr. Brown find out the final score?
6. Which teams played in the most recent Rose Bowl?
7. Can you find some other Bowl games?

Debate Corner Us Groups

1. In your group (4 or 5 people), choose one of the propositions below.

- Sport develops our minds and bodies.
- Winning isn't everything.
- The Olympic Games have lost the original spirit.
- Professional sportspeople are paid way too much.

2. Choose one pair (Pro) to agree with your proposition, one pair (Con) to disagree with it, and (if there are 5 people in your group) one person to be the Timekeeper.

Pro/Con Pair, Speaker 1:
▶ These phrases will help you present your arguments.

What I'm saying is …	Let me put it another way.	For this reason …
I'm saying that …	Don't misunderstand me.	Owing to this, …
The point is that …	What I'm trying to say is …	This is why …
I'm talking about …	That's not what I said.	Therefore …
What I mean is …	That's not what I meant.	As a result …
Don't get me wrong.	Let's get it straight.	Consequently …

Pro/Con Pair, Speaker 2
▶ These phrases will help you to reject the other team's arguments.

What do you mean?	What are you trying to say?	That may be so, but …
How do you mean?	Can you explain why …?	That may be true, but …
In what way?	Why do you think that?	You may be right, but …
Why do you say that?	You can't mean that!	Possibly, but …
Why is that?	Do you really think that?	What bothers me is …
Come off it!	That's ridiculous!	What I don't like is …

Timekeeper: These phrases will help you control the debate.

Today's proposition is …	Speaking for the proposition is ….
You have two minutes to speak.	Speaking against the proposition is ….
Your time is up.	The next speaker is …
Next speaker please.	The proposition has been accepted.
Your conclusions please.	The proposition has been rejected.

Let's Debate!

1 **Pro Pair:** Write three reasons for agreeing with the proposition, plus your conclusion.

2 **Con Pair:** Write three reasons for disagreeing with the proposition, plus your conclusion.

3 **Timekeeper:** Look at pages 70 and 72 and think of how you will start and end the debate.

First of all, …
_____
_____
_____

Next, …
_____
_____
_____

Furthermore, …
_____
_____
_____

In conclusion, …
_____
_____
_____

There are some sample arguments on the next page.

Let's Begin! Us Groups

Timekeeper:

1. Start the debate (see pages 70 and 72).

2. Ask the first Pro speaker to state the 'Pro' arguments.
   Tell him/her that he/she has 2 minutes.

3. Ask the first Con speaker to state the 'Con' arguments.
   Tell him/her that he/she has 2 minutes.

4. Ask the second Pro student to speak and give his/her conclusions.
   Tell him/her that he/she has 2 minutes.

5. Ask the second Con student to speak and give his/her conclusions.
   Tell him/her that he/she has 2 minutes.

6. End the debate (see pages 70 and 72). Either you can decide which team had the best arguments, or you can ask another group to decide.

Debate Sample Us Groups

- Listen to the debate sample on Track 32 on the CD-Rom.
- These are some ideas (only Pro 1 and Con 1), to help you get started.
- The proposition is "Professional sportspeople are paid way too much."
- Can you find phrases from page 70 here?

Timekeeper: Today's debate is on the proposition "Professional sportspeople are paid way too much." Speaker one for the Pro Team, please give your arguments in favor of the proposition. You have two minutes.

Pro Speaker 1: I am in favor of the proposition. The point is that sport is too commercialized these days. What I'm talking about is massive sponsorship by companies. For this reason sports stars earn huge amounts of money. As a result this leads to drug taking, betting and even corruption. Don't get me wrong, I love sport, but what I'm saying is that the original spirit of friendly competition is dead. What I mean is winning is everything now, whereas sport should be about participation and fair play.

Timekeeper: Thank you. Now I call upon Speaker one for the Con Team. Please give your rebuttal of ProSpeaker 1's arguments. You have two minutes.

Con Speaker 1: Pro Speaker has a point, but what bothers me is that she is being too negative. Let's get it straight. Sports professionals work hard and their jobs are very stressful. If they get injured or reach thirty years old, their career can be over. Don't misunderstand me. I know some players take drugs, but these are just a small minority. The majority are honest people who give us great entertainment. It's ridiculous to say they earn too much. Do you really think that? They deserve every penny.

Timekeeper: Thank you. Now I call upon the audience. You have heard the arguments for and against the proposition that professional sports people are paid way too much. All in favor of the proposition, please raise your hands. All those against the proposition, please raise your hands. I now declare that the proposition has been accepted/rejected.

Further Reading: There are more debate links and interesting activities at www.inkbooks.co.kr.

9 Fashion

Brainstorming

- What do you think of brand clothes? Are they really better than other clothes?
- How many fashion brands can you think of?

Task 1
- Write the names and colors of the clothes that these models are wearing.
- What about their hair? What color is it? How long is it?

Task 2

Student A:
- Walk from one side of the room to the other side.
- Walk slowly, one foot in front of the other, like a fashion model.

Student B:
- Tell everyone what Student A is wearing.
- Imitate a fashion announcer. Here is an example:

"Ladies and gentlemen, Ji-hye is wearing black ankle length boots and black tights. She is wearing jean-style hot-pants below a red woolen sweater. She has a silver necklace outside of the sweater. Ji-hye is a brunette and her wavy hair comes to below her shoulders."

Eco-fashion

- Listen to Track 33 on the CD-Rom.
- Read this passage together.
- While you read, match the words and phrases at the bottom of the page.
- Then answer the questions on the next page.

The world of fashion has changed greatly over the years and now, in the 21st century, it is involved in important social, environmental and commercial issues. Because of these, we are being advised to buy eco-friendly, ethical fashion, rather than shopping for clothes that just look good.

A number of fashion issues have arisen in recent years. First, many women have a poor body image and even eating problems because they want to be like the thin fashion models. Second, the fur industry is known for its inhumane treatment of animals. Third, the new fashions that come out every year encourage people to buy clothes that they don't need. Then there is the effect on the environment, as well as the use of child labor in some developing countries.

Because of these and other issues, fashion designers now want to maximize the benefit to the people who make the clothes and help to reduce poverty. They also want to minimize the impact on the environment through 'sustainable fashion'. This means considering the environmental and social impact of the clothes, including their 'carbon footprint'.

Eco-friendly clothes last for a long time, they use fewer chemicals and pesticides, and they are made from natural materials and dyes. So next time you buy new clothes, take a moment to look at the label and see if they are eco-friendly. You can support people in poorer communities as well as help to preserve the environment.

Match the words and phrases on the left to the definitions on the right.

eco-friendly	a major influence or effect
ethical	able to last for a long time
issue	an important subject or topic
body image	chemicals used to kill insects that damage plants
inhumane	increase as much as possible
impact	make as small as possible
maximize	morally right or good
minimize	not environmentally harmful
sustainable	not kind or gentle to people or animals
carbon footprint	the amount of greenhouse gases caused by a product
pesticide	the picture we have of our appearance

There are more reading passages at www.inkbooks.co.kr

Comprehension Check

1. What is ethical fashion?
2. What is sustainable fashion?
3. What fashion issues have arisen lately?
4. What is the fashion industry doing about these problems?
5. How can we support people in poorer communities?
6. Summarize the final paragraph in one sentence.

Think for Yourself

- [ ] What are the social issues involving fashion?
- [ ] What are the commercial issues?
- [ ] What is sweatshop labor?
- [ ] Do you know any eco-friendly brands?
- [ ] What does "Green is the new black" mean?

Background Information

Did you know?

- [ ] For Egyptian women in 1500 B.C.E, a shaved head was the height of beauty.
- [ ] Buttons on men's shirts are on the right. On women's blouses they are on the left.
- [ ] Two out of five women in America dye their hair.
- [ ] Fashionable people in England in the 19th century used only blue or green silk umbrellas.
- [ ] Fashion designer Ralph Lauren's first job was selling gloves.
- [ ] Calvin Klein designs clothes for Julia Roberts, Gwyneth Paltrow, and Helen Hunt.
- [ ] Tommy Hilfiger's first store, in upstate New York, was called "The People's Place."
- [ ] Yves Saint Laurent, the 'King of Fashion,' was the first designer to put his fashion show live on the Internet.
- [ ] According to Earth Pledge, "At least 8,000 chemicals are used to turn raw materials into textiles and 25% of the world's pesticides are used to grow non-organic cotton."

Discussion Us Groups

- Talk together about the questions below.
- Use the Conversation Strategies at the bottom of the page.

1 Do you follow trends and fashions?
- Yes : Why?
- No : Why not?

2 Do you buy fashionable clothes each year?
- Yes : What happens to the old clothes?
- No : Why not?

3 Do you prefer 'brand' clothes?
- Yes : Why? What is the attraction?
- No : Why not?

4 Talk about a fashionable person.
- Would you like to be like that person?

5 Can you tell someone's personality by their clothes?
- Give some examples.

6 What colors are in fashion this year?
- Do you like them?

7 What do you think of fashion shows?

8 Would you like to be a fashion model?
- Explain your answer.

9 Would you like to be a fashion designer?
- Explain your answer.

10 What do you think about eco-fashion?
- Do you buy sustainable fashion?

Conversation Strategies

Asking for an opinion:

I'd like to ask …
Can I ask you …?
Could you tell me …?
What do you think about …?
What's your opinion?
How do you feel?

Sharing opinions:

Of course!
Certainly.
I'll be happy to tell you.
Well, in my opinion, …
To tell the truth,
Frankly speaking,

Dialogue

- Listen to Track 34 on the CD-Rom.
- Read the dialogue with your partner.
- Perform the dialogue together.
- Change roles. Perform the dialogue again.

Ji-hye	Excuse me, Mrs. Brown.
Mrs. Brown	Hello, Ji-hye. How can I help you?
Ji-hye	I want to ask you about my new outfit.
Mrs. Brown	Let's have a look. Turn around a bit.
Ji-hye	What do you think? Is it me?
Mrs. Brown	Certainly! In fact it's out of this world.
Ji-hye	In a good way, or a bad way?
Mrs. Brown	Don't be silly! In a good way, of course! When did you get it?
Ji-hye	Yesterday. My old clothes were getting worn out, so I decided to get some new ones.
Mrs. Brown	Well, I think they suit you down to the ground.
Ji-hye	Thanks, Mrs. Brown.
Mrs. Brown	But why ask me? Why don't you ask Jenny?
Ji-hye	Jenny is my friend. She'd say anything to make me feel good.
Mrs. Brown	You mean I wouldn't?
Ji-hye	No, that's not it. I mean I can trust you to mean what you say.

Key Words and Expressions

outfit
suit of clothes; matching clothes

"is it me?"
"Does it suit me and my personality?"

out of this world
unique; original; fantastic

"Don't be silly!"
"Are you joking?"

worn out
old; in a bad condition

down to the ground
100%; absolutely; completely

Dialogue Quiz

1. Why did Ji-hye buy her new outfit?
2. Why didn't she show it to Jenny straight away?
3. Does Jenny always mean what she says?
4. Does Mrs. Brown like Ji-hye's outfit?
5. Do you think Ji-hye's clothes are eco-friendly?
6. Do you say what you mean, or do you mean what you say?
7. Do you eat to live, or do you live to eat?

Let's Make a Role-play!

- **Situation 1**: A customer is trying on shoes in a shoe shop or department store.
- **Situation 2**: A customer is trying on clothes in a clothes shop or department store.

1. Choose your role (customer, shop assistant).
2. Read your role-card and your hints.
3. Think about what you will say in the role-play.
4. Write your ideas on the next page.

Customer

Here are your hints:

1. Enter the shop.
2. Tell the assistant what you are looking for.
3. Explain your size and the color you want.
4. Try on some shoes/clothes.
5. Try some other shoes/clothes.
6. Find some shoes/clothes that you like.
7. Ask the price.
8. Either buy them or leave the shop.

Here are some phrases you can use.

- I'm looking for ..... .
- I'm not sure of my size.
- I used to be size …
- Do you have these in (color)?
- Have you got something in (color)?
- Can I try it[them] on?
- Is[Are] it[they] eco-friendly?
- It's[They're] too big/small.
- The color is too strong.
- It's[They're] not really me.
- What do you think?
- It's[They're] just right.
- How much is[are] it[they]?
- Can I have a discount?
- I'll take it[them].
- Here is my card.
- Thank you. Goodbye.

Shop assistant

Here are your hints:

1. Greet the customer.
2. Ask him/her what he/she is looking for.
3. Ask about size and color.
4. Get some shoes/clothes.
5. Help the customer try them on.
6. Tell the customer the price.
7. Sell the shoes/clothes.
8. Thank the customer.

Here are some useful phrases:

- Good morning/afternoon/evening.
- Can I help you?
- What is your size?
- What color would you like?
- We don't have that color.
- How about this one[these]?
- Do you want to try it[them] on?
- How about a bigger[smaller] size?
- It[They] looks[look] good on you.
- The color matches your eyes.
- I can give you a discount.
- Do you have a (shop name) card?
- Thank you for shopping with us.
- See you again.

Role-play Script

- With your partner, make a storyboard for your role-play.
- Perform your role-play together.
- Now perform it to another group.

Time to Reflect!

- Fill in this self-assessment and think about your contribution to the role-play.
- Then add your comments. How was your role-play? Did you do your best?

5 = Absolutely, 4 = Yes, 3 = Sort of, 2 = Not really, 1 = "Not at all"

	Role-play self-assessment	5	4	3	2	1
1	I contributed to choosing the title.					
2	I contributed to making the plot (story).					
3	I contributed to drawing the pictures.					
4	I contributed to writing the words.					
5	I rehearsed the role-play with my partner.					
6	We performed the role-play to another pair.					
7	Our drama took a reasonable amount of time.					
8	Our drama was interesting.					
9	I used expressive body language.					
10	I was confident and cheerful.					

Total = _____ /50

My comments:
....
....
....

Now review what you have done in this Unit and prepare for the next Unit.

Review
Browse the website for Unit 9.

Preview
Browse the website for Unit 10.

Prepare
Look at the activities in Unit 10.

10 Dream Jobs

> Choose a job you love, and you'll never work a day in your life. (Confucius)

> Your time is limited, so don't waste it living someone else's life. (Steve Jobs)

> Dare to live the life you have dreamed for yourself. Go forward and make your dreams come true. (Ralph Waldo Emerson)

What's My Line? Us Groups

1. **Student A:** Choose an occupation from Table 1.
   - Don't tell anyone what it is.
   - Stand up and perform your occupation.
2. **Everybody else:** Watch Student A's performance.
   - Ask up to 10 questions from Table 2.
   - See if you can guess the occupation.

Table 1

actor	fashion model	police officer	soldier
bank teller	flight attendant	professor	student
chef	judge	reporter	taxi driver
dancer	mailman	scientist	teacher
dentist	musician	secretary	tennis player
doctor	nurse	singer	TV anchor
farmer	pilot	soccer player	waitress

Table 2

Do you start work at 9 a.m.?	Do you work in a factory?
Do you use a computer?	Do you work in a post office?
Do you use special tools?	Do you work in a restaurant?
Do you wear special clothes?	Do you work in a shop?
Do you wear a uniform?	Do you work in an office?
Do you work alone?	Do you work indoors?
Do you work at night?	Do you work on Sundays?
Do you work in a bank?	Do you work with animals?
Do you work in a plane?	Do you work with food?

Right-brain Jobs

- Listen to Track 35 on the CD-Rom.
- Read this passage together.
- While you read, match the words and phrases at the bottom of the page.
- Then answer the questions on the next page.

Parents used to want their children to become doctors, lawyers, accountants or engineers. These have always been jobs that lead to a prosperous life. However, tomorrow's economies will reward a different kind of mind. Instead of left-brain knowledge workers, the future belongs to right-brained artists, inventors, and designers.

Our brains are divided into two hemispheres. The left one is logical. It works like a computer. The right one is artistic, controlling creativity, emotions and motivation. We use both sides of our brain in daily life, but right hemisphere abilities are becoming more valuable for professional people like graphic designers, psychologists, interior designers, and managers.

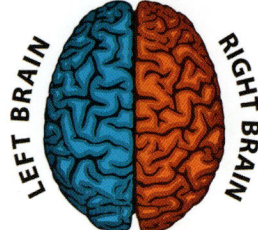

Why is this happening? Firstly, products have to be more than just useful these days. They must also be attractive and meaningful. Secondly, knowledge-based jobs are being outsourced to places like India and the Philippines. Finally, computers can do left-brain jobs much faster, cheaper and often better than people can.

Future jobs won't just be "high-tech." They will also be "high-concept." This means creating artistic designs and using unusual ideas to make new products. So next time your parents ask what you want to be in the future, how about saying that you are considering a right-brain career path?

Match the words and phrases on the left to the definitions on the right.

prosperous	beautiful; pretty; nice-looking
inventor	deep, expressive, worthwhile
hemisphere	half of a sphere
ability	idea; notion
product	long-term occupation; profession
attractive	someone who makes new things
meaningful	something made by humans or machines
outsourced	the power or skill to do something
concept	sent away to be done in a different country
career	wealthy; comfortable; well-off

Comprehension Check

1. Which jobs are traditionally the best career paths?
2. Are these left-brain or right-brain jobs?
3. Do we use our right-brain in every day activities?
4. Why are knowledge-based jobs becoming less valuable?
5. What is the difference between 'high-tech' and 'high-concept'?
6. Can 'high-concept' jobs be outsourced?
7. Can you find another phrase that means 'left-brain jobs' in the passage?
8. Why does this passage suggest considering a right-brain career path?

Think for Yourself

- [ ] Are you aiming for a left-brain or a right-brain job?
- [ ] Why are jobs outsourced?
- [ ] What is your dream job?
- [ ] If you could make your own company, what would it be?
- [ ] If you could invent something, what would it be?

Background Information

Did you know?

- [ ] Here are some right-brain jobs: sand sculptor, Internet entrepreneur, race car driver, idea guru, pop star, restaurant critic, pro athlete, fashion photographer, travel journalist, and movie star
- [ ] Here are some left-brain jobs: scientist, lawyer, civil engineer, accountant, computer programmer.
- [ ] The right brain controls muscles on the left side of the body.
- [ ] The left brain controls muscles on the right side of the body.
- [ ] Right-brain functions include awareness of space, intuition, music, art and rhythm, as well as visual aspects.
- [ ] Left-brain functions include speech and language, logical analysis and reasoning, and mathematical abilities.
- [ ] Right brain personality traits include creative, artistic and open-minded holistic thinking and intuitive reasoning. A "whole to details" approach.
- [ ] Left-brain personality traits include analytical, logical thinking, focusing on detail. A "details to the whole" approach.

Discussion Groups

- Talk together about the questions below.
- Use the Conversation Strategies at the bottom of the page.

1 What is your dream job?
  ▶ Discuss your future careers together.

2 What do you want from a career?
  ▶ Which is more important: money, security, happiness, or challenge?

3 What do your parents want you to do?
  ▶ Will you respect their wishes?

4 Do you want to stay in one job for your whole life?
  ▶ Why? Why not? Support your opinion.

5 Is it OK to be unemployed?
  ▶ Why? Why not? Support your opinion.

6 Would you like to start your own business?
  ▶ Why? Why not? Support your opinion.

7 What do you think of outsourcing?
  ▶ Are many jobs being outsourced from Korea?
  ▶ Where are they going to?

8 Will computers take over many jobs in the future?
  ▶ What sorts of jobs do robots do now?
  ▶ Can computers think like human beings?
  ▶ What will happen to people who lose their jobs to computers and robots?

Conversation Strategies

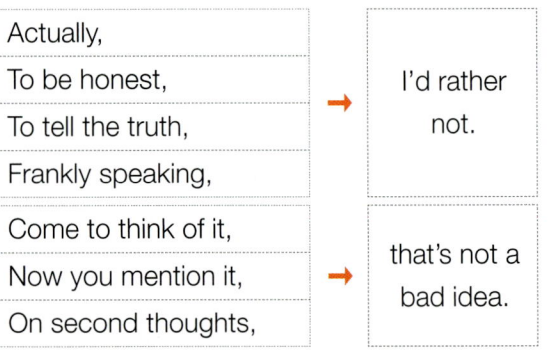

Dialogue Us pairs

- Listen to Track 36 on the CD-Rom.
- Read the dialogue with your partner.
- Perform the dialogue together.
- Change roles. Perform the dialogue again.

Key Words and Expressions

chat
brief talk

"I can't see it happening."
"I don't think it's possible."

media design
3D animation, graphic design, digital media

"We don't want to push you."
"We don't want to force you to make a decision."

"I see what you mean."
"I see your point."
"I understand."

(Mrs. Brown is making dinner.
Kevin comes into the kitchen for a glass of juice.)

Kevin	Hi, mum. That smells good!
Mrs. Brown	Oh, Kevin. While you're here, can we have a chat?
Kevin	Of course, mum. What is it? *(He gets the juice out of the refrigerator.)*
Mrs. Brown	Your dad and I have been talking about you.
Kevin	Oh dear. Have I done something wrong?
Mrs. Brown	Don't worry. We were talking about your future. Do you have any plans?
Kevin	I'd love to be a film director, but I can't see it happening.
Mrs. Brown	Anything else?
Kevin	I haven't really thought about it. What do you think?
Mrs. Brown	Well, you always get good grades in art and media.
Kevin	Hmm, and I do like photography. *(He drinks the juice.)*
Mrs. Brown	We don't want to push you, but …
Kevin	Yes, you're right. Maybe I'll be a photographer.
Mrs. Brown	In that case, you need to study photography and media design in college.
Kevin	I see what you mean.
Mrs. Brown	We want what's best for you, after all.
Kevin	Thanks, mum. Now, when's dinner?

Dialogue Quiz

1. Why did Kevin come into the kitchen?
2. What does Mrs. Brown want to talk to him about?
3. What is Kevin's dream job?
4. Why does Kevin consider being a photographer? (2 reasons)
5. Do Kevin's parents have their own plans for his career?
6. What would you say to Kevin if you were Mrs. Brown?

Debate Corner Groups

1. In your group (4 or 5 people), choose one of the propositions below.

- Everyone should try for his or her dream job.
- Technology should not replace human labor.
- A successful career is more important than a happy family life.
- College majors should be more career-focused.

2. Choose one pair (Pro) to agree with your proposition, one pair (Con) to disagree with it, and (if there are 5 people in your group) one person to be the Timekeeper.

Pro/Con Pair, Speaker 1:
▶ These phrases will help you present your arguments strongly:

In my opinion	I'm sure that …	Clearly, …
In my view	I'm certain that …	Obviously
I strongly believe that	I'm pretty sure that …	There's no doubt that …
I definitely think that	According to statistics,	Without doubt, …
Well, if you ask me, …	Actually, …	Undoubtedly
Well, I think …	In fact, …	Surely

Pro/Con Pair, Speaker 2
▶ These phrases will help you to make your conclusions:

Generally, …	To put it simply,	To summarize, …
As a rule, …	So, in short, …	To make a long story short, …
Typically, …	All in all, …	To put it in a few words, …
By and large,…	In the end, …	In a nutshell, …
On average, …	To conclude, …	In brief, …
Generally speaking, …	To sum up, …	To be brief, …

Timekeeper: These phrases will help you control the debate.

Today's proposition is …	Speaking for the proposition is ….
You have two minutes to speak.	Speaking against the proposition is ….
Your time is up.	The next speaker is …
Next speaker please.	The proposition has been accepted.
Your conclusions please.	The proposition has been rejected.

Let's Debate!

① **Pro Pair:** Look at pages 62, 70 and 86 for debate language and phrases.
Then write three reasons for agreeing with the proposition, plus your conclusion.

② **Con Pair:** Look at pages 62, 70 and 86 for debate language and phrases.
Then write three reasons for disagreeing with the proposition, plus your conclusion.

③ **Timekeeper:** Look at page 86 and think of how you will start and end the debate.

First of all, ...
_____
_____
_____

Next, ...
_____
_____
_____

Furthermore, ...
_____
_____
_____

In conclusion, ...
_____
_____
_____

There are some sample arguments on the next page.

Let's Begin! Us Groups

Timekeeper:

1. Start the debate (see pages 72 and 86).

2. Ask the first Pro speaker to state the 'Pro' arguments.
   Tell him/her that he/she has 2 minutes.

3. Ask the first Con speaker to state the 'Con' arguments.
   Tell him/her that he/she has 2 minutes.

4. Ask the second Pro student to speak and give his/her conclusions.
   Tell him/her that he/she has 2 minutes.

5. Ask the second Con student to speak and give his/her conclusions.
   Tell him/her that he/she has 2 minutes.

6. End the debate. Either you can decide which team had the best arguments, or you can ask another group to decide. If there is an audience, you can put the proposition to the vote (page 86).

Argument Samples  Groups

- Here are two samples to give you some ideas (Tracks 37 and 38).
- They are about the proposition "Everyone should try for his or her dream job".
- Can you find phrases from page 86 in these samples?

Pro Speaker 1: I am in favor of the proposition. I strongly believe that we should follow our dreams. What's the use of doing the same thing every day for the rest of your life? If you ask me, that's too high a price to pay for security. Obviously, I'm going to find a job I love doing. It might not be well-paid, but I'm pretty sure that money isn't everything. If I can use my talents to make high-concept products, then there's no doubt that I'll be successful, and enjoy a happy family life.

Con Speaker 1: To summarize, the most important thing is to get a secure job and settle down. By and large, being a public official or a teacher is good. Typically, you can keep the same job for your whole life and get a pension at the end of it. Undoubtedly it won't be exciting or challenging, but in the end your family doesn't have to worry about where the next meal is coming from. To conclude, I am against the proposition. To put it in a few words, job security is more important than following your dream.

Brain Puzzle

- Let's find out whether you are a left-brain or right-brain thinker.
- Look at the words below and say the colors, not the words.
- Your right brain will try to say the color; your left brain will read the word!
- Can you do it in less than a minute?

If this is easy for you, your right-brain is dominant. If you cannot do this in one minute, your left-brain is dominant.

RED BLUE BLACK RED
ORANGE BLACK BLUE
WHITE BLUE GREEN
BLUE ORANGE WHITE
GREEN BLUE PINK
WHITE ORANGE RED

11 Well-being

The Well-being Survey

Situation: You are conducting a survey about people's lifestyles.
1. Exchange books with your partner.
2. Interview your partner using the survey form below.
3. Change the statements into questions ("*Do you know what you want to do in your life?*")

#	Statement	Left	1	2	3	4	5	Right
1	I know what I want to do in my life.	False	1				5	True
2	I find it easy to concentrate.	False	1				5	True
3	I make my own quiet time every day.	False	1				5	True
4	I do some exercise or deep breathing every day.	False	1				5	True
5	I eat organic food whenever I can.	False	1				5	True
6	During most of the day, my energy level is …	very low	1	2	3	4	5	very high
7	On the whole, my life is …	boring	1	2	3	4	5	exciting
8	I feel happiness in my heart …	never	1	2	3	4	5	all the time
9	My life so far has been …	unproductive	1	2	3	4	5	productive
10	I feel that my school studies are …	worthless	1	2	3	4	5	worthwhile
11	When I am frightened, …	I get nervous.	1	2	3	4	5	I stay calm.
12	When I think about my past, I feel …	regrets	1	2	3	4	5	no regrets
	Total							

Now give your partner feedback from the Answer key at the end of the book.

Well-being School Lunches

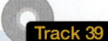

- Listen to Track 39 on the CD-Rom.
- Read this passage together.
- While you read, match the words and phrases at the bottom of the page.
- Then answer the questions on the next page.

 Groups

Did you know that school children consume more than a third of their daily food at school? This makes school a great place to establish healthy eating patterns. *Falling in Love with Food* is the name of the annual National Nutrition Week in Australia, when 'healthy lunch' activity kits are given to schools. These kits include information about the health value of foods and hints about how to make well-being lunch boxes containing all the 5 food types.

In addition to this week-long event, *Let's Get Fruity* is an exciting new program in Australian primary schools, supported by the kiwifruit industry of New Zealand. It provides lots of fun classroom activities and other materials, all of which explain the importance of fruit and water. School children often like high-fat cookies and candies, but these do not provide the energy needed for studying. Because of this, one of the first changes made by the *Let's Get Fruity* program is to introduce a 'fruit and water time' during classroom lessons.

Many people are worried about the rising number of overweight children in Australia, and fruit offers a low calorie, nutritious snack. Eating more fruit can improve children's health and well-being, and there are other benefits as well. It has been said that if every Australian ate one extra fruit a day, 180 million *Australian Dollars would be saved in national health care costs. As the saying goes, "An apple a day keeps the doctor away"!

*1 Australian Dollar = 840 Korean Won

Match the words and phrases on the left to the definitions on the right.

consume	a collection of activities
establish	a unit of energy value
activity kit	food eaten between meals
exciting	healthy; valuable
introduce	to begin; start
overweight	to eat; use up
calorie	to make better
nutritious	to set up; make
snack	too heavy
improve	very interesting

90 Active English Discussion 1

There are more reading passages at www.inkbooks.co.kr

Comprehension Check

1. Why is school a good place to start good eating habits?
2. How often does National Nutrition Week happen?
3. What's wrong with high-fat snacks?
4. Name a change made by the 'Let's Get Fruity' program.
5. How can eating fruit help overweight school children?
6. How can eating fruit help the economy of Australia?

Think for Yourself

- [ ] Do you have healthy eating patterns?
- [ ] Have you heard of the 'food pyramid'?
- [ ] What are the 5 food types?
- [ ] Why do you think the New Zealand kiwifruit industry is supporting the Australian schools fruit program?

Background Information

Here are some tips for a healthy lifestyle:

- [ ] **Eat well**: Cut down on high-fat foods. Your body is your temple and you are what you eat.
- [ ] **Be active**: All forms of exercise are good, even walking.
- [ ] **Sleep well**: Sleep is really important, especially for young people. This is when your body does most of its growing.
- [ ] **Express yourself**: Don't hide your feelings. It takes lot of energy and it is stressful. Let your feelings come out.
- [ ] **Relax**: Make time to relax with friends. Forget your worries and do whatever makes you feel good. Be kind to yourself.
- [ ] **Don't be fooled**: Don't fall for the latest diet on TV. The best way to lose weight is to eat healthily and to be active!
- [ ] **Reduce stress**: Make sure you have 5 minutes every hour to stretch, take a walk, or just close your eyes.
- [ ] **Breathe**: Try some deep breathing with the whole lungs. Breathe in and out slowly. Get lots of oxygen into your body!

Discussion Groups

- Talk together about the questions below.
- Use the Conversation Strategies at the bottom of the page.

1. **Do you already do the tips on the previous page?**
   ▶ Can you think of some other tips?
2. **Why is well-being so popular these days?**
3. **What is well-being food?**
   ▶ How is it different from other food?
4. **What is organic food?**
   ▶ How about brain food?
   ▶ How about detox food?
5. **What do you think of vegetarians?**
   ▶ How about vegans or fruitarians?
   ▶ Explain your opinion.
6. **Does physical exercise affect mental health?**
   ▶ Explain your opinion.
7. **What do you think of pilates and yoga?**
   ▶ Explain your opinion.
8. **Is your life stressful?**
   ▶ How can we reduce stress in our lives?
9. **What do you think about meditation?**
   ▶ Is it helpful?
10. **What do you think about dieting?**

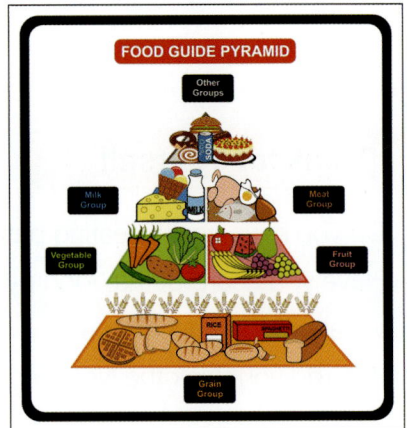

Conversation Strategies

Suggesting:

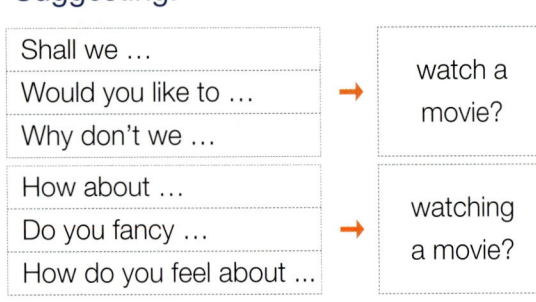

| Shall we … |
| Would you like to … |
| Why don't we … |

→ watch a movie?

| How about … |
| Do you fancy … |
| How do you feel about … |

→ watching a movie?

Saying 'no' politely:

| Actually, I'm not into … |
| Well, I'm not keen on … |
| I'm not really interested in … |

→ watching movies.

| I'm not in the mood for … |
| I'd rather not. |
| Maybe another time. |
| I'd love to, but not today. |
| Some other time, perhaps. |

Dialogue

- Listen to Track 40 on the CD-Rom.
- Read the dialogue with your partners.
- Perform the dialogue together.
- Change roles. Perform the dialogue again.

(Jenny and Ji-hye are reading a magazine on the floor, while Grandma Brown is vacuuming the room.)

Grandma Brown	Hello, you two. Can you move a little bit?
Jenny	Sure, Grandma.
Grandma Brown	Thanks. I won't be a minute.

(Jenny and Ji-hye move onto the sofa and read the magazine.)

Ji-hye	I really like this healthy food section.
Jenny	Me too. And how about the Organic Diet on the next page?
Ji-hye	I've heard lots of Hollywood stars are into it.
Jenny	Yes. It must be good.
Grandma Brown	*(She has finished vacuuming.)* What's that you're reading?
Ji-hye	It's the latest edition of TeenYoung Magazine.
Grandma Brown	You don't believe in diets, do you?
Jenny	Of course we do, Grandma.
Grandma Brown	Don't be silly. You're still growing up.
Ji-hye	But we want to be cool, and wear the latest fashion.
Grandma Brown	I see. Well, if you really want to lose weight, you can help me with the housework.
Jenny	We'd love to, Grandma, but …
Ji-hye	Don't we have some homework to do?
Jenny	Yes, that's right. We have to go. Ciao!

Key Words and Expressions

"I won't be a minute."
"I'll be very quick."

"You don't believe in diets, do you?"
"Do you really think that diets are good for you?"

housework
cleaning the house, washing clothes, doing the washing up, etc.

"Ciao!"
"Goodbye!"

Dialogue Quiz

1. Why does Grandma Brown ask the two girls to move?
2. What age group is the magazine aimed at?
3. Why does Jenny expect the diet to be good?
4. Why do the two girls want to go on a diet?
5. What does Grandma Brown suggest?
6. What do Jenny and Ji-hye think about her suggestion?

Unit 11 Well-being 93

Let's Make a Role-play!

- **Situation 1**: A patient is visiting the doctor.
- **Situation 2**: A patient is visiting a dietician.

1. Choose your role (patient, doctor, nutritionist).
2. Read your role-card and your hints.
3. Think about what you will say in the role-play.
4. Make a script on the next page.

Patient

I can't sleep at night.	I feel tired all the time.	I feel depressed.
I can't concentrate.	I can't remember things.	I feel dizzy when I get up.
I can't get up in the morning.	My clothes don't fit me anymore.	There is a strange noise in my ears.
I just want to cry.	I don't have any energy.	I'm putting on weight.
I feel stressed out.	I get angry for no reason.	I get migraines.

Doctor

When did you first notice this?	How long has it been like this?	How often does it happen?
Are you busy at work?	Do you have a lot of stress?	Has anything happened to you lately?
You need some exercise.	You need to change your diet.	You need to stop smoking.
You need to rest.	Go to bed for a few days.	You should see a dietician.
You are working too hard.	You need to relax.	Walk or cycle to work.

Dietician

What do you eat in the morning?	What do you eat for lunch?	What do you eat for dinner?
Do you eat snacks?	Do you drink soft drinks?	Do you drink alchohol?
Do you smoke?	Do you exercise regularly?	I will make a diet plan for you.
You need to change your diet.	You need more protein.	You should eat less carbohydrates.
You should cut down on fatty foods.	How many hours do you sleep at night?	Come back in a month.

Role-play Script

- With your partner, make a script for your role-play.
- Perform your role-play together.
- Now perform it to another group.

Title:

Characters:

Location:

Brain Teasers

- Can you solve these puzzles?
- The answers are in the Answer section at the back of the book.

1 What is the number of the restaurant table with the plates on it?

16   06   68   88   98

2 You enter a room. You have only one match to start a kerosene lamp, an oil heater, and a wood-burning stove. Which would you light first and why?

3 Two men played chess. They played five games, and each man won three games. How do you explain this?

Time to Reflect!

- Fill in this self-assessment and think about your personal qualities.
- There are no correct answers. Just write about yourself.

	Words and sentences that describe me
Health	
Exercise	
Values	
Emotions and feelings	
Beliefs	
Needs	

There are more puzzles and other activities on the website at www.inkbooks.co.kr

12 Travel in Korea

Brainstorming

- Have you been to many places in Korea?
- What is your favorite place? How many times have you been there?

Task

- Solve this Travel-in-Korea crossword together.
- If you don't know how to spell the words, look in the Reading passage (next page).

Clues Across

1. This is the house in which the president lives.
5. This is an ancient school near Andong.
6. There is a cherry-blossom festival here every year.
8. This is the tallest building in Seoul.
10. This city is the ancient capital of Silla.
11. This famous mountain is in Gangwon-do.
12. Many foreigners buy Korean souvenirs here.
13. This river passes through Seoul.
14. This is a national park in the north of Seoul.
15. This city held an EXPO in 1993.

Clues Down

2. This palace is also called 'The Northern Palace.'
3. This city holds an annual Mask Dance Festival.
4. This island is the most popular tourist destination in Korea.
7. This is a famous market in Seoul.
9. This is a famous temple in Gyeongju.

*The answers are in the Answer Key, at the back of the book.

What's number 1 across? What's number 2 down?
What do you think? I don't know. I'm not sure.
Let's look it up. How do you spell it?
What did you say? One more time, please.

Travel in Korea

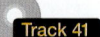

- Listen to Track 41 on the CD-Rom.
- Read this passage together.
- While you read, match the words and phrases at the bottom of the page.
- Then answer the questions on the next page.

Korea has its own special culture, which visitors can experience in the cuisine, arts and crafts, temples, festivals, mountains, and all the charming tourist attractions of the peninsula.

There are many wonderful places waiting to be discovered in the 'Land of the Morning Calm.' For instance, the number one tourist destination is Jeju-do, known for its 'Three Abundances' (wind, women, and rocks). Next, there is Mt. Seoraksan, famous for the color of the leaves in fall. For visitors who want to visit an ancient school, there is Dosanseowon, near Andong, the home of the annual Mask Dance festival. But that's not all. Jinhae holds a cherry-blossom festival every year, Gyeongju (the ancient capital of Silla) has Bulguksa temple and the World Cultural Expo, and we can still visit the site of Daejeon Expo '93.

We can also experience the magic of Korea without leaving Seoul. If we want some exercise, we can climb Mt. Bukhan, to the north of Seoul, or take a walk along the banks of the Hangang river. Gyeongbokgung Palace is well worth a visit, while Namdaemun lets us experience the atmosphere of an all-night market. Then there is the 63 Building, and Cheongwadae, the home of the president. Finally, visitors can find great souvenirs and Korean restaurants in Insadong.

To sum up, there are many sights and sounds to be experienced, both for visitors and those who were born here. For the former, every moment brings new cultural surprises. For the latter, there is the proverb, 'East, west, home's best.'

Match the words and phrases on the left to the definitions on the right.

cuisine	a large amount of something
crafts	an area of land with sea on three sides
tourist attractions	charm, attractiveness
peninsula	first person mentioned
abundance	items made by skilled people
Mt.	last person mentioned
magic	Mount; mountain
atmosphere	places that tourists find interesting
souvenir	reminder; memento; token
former	style of cooking
latter	the feeling of a place

Comprehension Check

1. How can tourists experience the culture of Korea?
2. Can you find another word for 'tourist' in the passage?
3. What is Mt. Seoraksan famous for?
4. What is Dosanseowon?
5. Has Seoul always been the capital of Korea?
6. Why do tourists visit Insadong?

Taesik Park / Shutterstock.com

Think for Yourself

☐ Why is Korean cuisine unique?
☐ What do you think 'Land of the Morning Calm' means?
☐ Can you explain the 'three abundances' of Jeju-do?
☐ How many festivals in Korea can you name?
☐ How is Korean culture changing?

Background Information

Did you know?

☐ The first dynasty in Korea was named Gojoseon and was founded by Dangun in 2333 BC.

☐ The name "Korea" comes from the Goryeo Dynasty.

☐ The highest point in South Korea is Mt. Hallasan in Jeju-do.

☐ 70% of the Korean peninsula is covered in mountains.

☐ Hangeul was introduced in 1446, by King Sejong.

☐ Printing from metal letters was developed in Korea before the Gutenberg printing press in Germany.

☐ Some of Korea's cities are among the most densely populated areas in the world.

☐ South Korea led the world in the use of high-speed broadband Internet access.

☐ The fountain in front of the Seoul World Cup Stadium was the world's highest fountain when it was built in 2002.

Discussion Groups

- Talk together about the questions below.
- Use the Conversation Strategies at the bottom of the page.

1. Why do tourists visit Korea?
- Is Korea a tourist-friendly country?
- Which tourist attractions would you recommend to tourists?

2. What do you know about culture shock?
- How might culture shock affect visitors to Korea?
- How might Korean tourists experience culture shock abroad?

3. Do you think Koreans should travel inside Korea before going abroad?
- Why? Why not? Support your opinion.

4. Is travel in Korea becoming too difficult these days?
- Are there too many cars on the roads?
- Are the tourist attractions overcrowded?

5. What do you think of traditional Korean culture?
- Respect for elders
- Male-dominated (patriarchal)

6. What do you think of modern Korean culture?
- Hallyu, fashion, K-Pop
- Korean movies, mini-series

7. Would you like to visit North Korea?
- Why? Why not? Support your opinion.
- Do you think North and South Korea will ever unify?

Conversation Strategies

Conversation Strategies:

Where are you going for the holidays?	Our plan is to …	go to Gyeongju.
	We'd like to …	
	We're hoping to …	
	We're going to …	
	We're planning to …	
	We're thinking of …	going to Gyeongju.
	If all goes well, we're …	
	What we have in mind is …	

Responding:

That's a great idea!
What a good idea!
That sounds great!
Fantastic!
I envy you!
Wonderful!
Have a great time.
Enjoy.

Dialogue

- Listen to Track 42 on the CD-Rom.
- Read the dialogue with your partners.
- Perform the dialogue together.
- Change roles. Perform the dialogue again.

(Dad and Jenny are sitting at the table, looking at a travel book.)

Mr. Brown	So what do you think, Jenny?
Jenny	How about starting in the capital?
Mr. Brown	You mean before we look at the rest of Korea?
Jenny	Yes. There are loads of attractions there.
Mr. Brown	OK. How long shall we stay?
Jenny	We could have a week in Seoul, and then another week or two touring Korea.
Mr. Brown	That sounds like a plan.
Jenny	I'd love to visit Gyeongju. There's so much to see there.
Mr. Brown	I know what you mean, but how about Jeju-do?
Jenny	Of course! And don't forget Seoraksan.
Mr. Brown	This is going to be some vacation!
Jenny	You're not kidding. I can't wait!

(Grandma Brown comes into the room.)

Grandma Brown	Hello. Have you made any plans yet?
Jenny	You bet, Grandma. We're thinking of going to Seoul first, and then Gyeongju, Jeju-do, Seoraksan, and lots of other places.
Grandma Brown	That sounds great. I wish I were going with you.
Mr. Brown	You can come another time, mum.
Grandma Brown	Of course. I'm happy to stay here and look after the house.

Key Words and Expressions

loads of attractions
many places to visit

"That sounds like a plan."
"That's a good idea."

"This is going to be some vacation!"
"This is going to be a wonderful vacation!"

"I can't wait!"
"I'm really looking forward to it!"

Dialogue Quiz

1. What sort of book are Jenny and Mr. Brown looking at?
2. What are they planning to do on their vacation?
3. Will everyone in the family go with them?
4. Will they tour the rest of Korea before looking at Seoul?
5. What will Grandma Brown do while they are away?
6. Where would you go if you had a three week vacation in Korea?

Debate Corner Us ▸ Groups

1. In your group (4 or 5 people), choose one of the propositions below.

- Tourism benefits the world.
- Koreans should explore Korea before traveling abroad.
- It is important to experience other cultures.
- East, west, home's best.

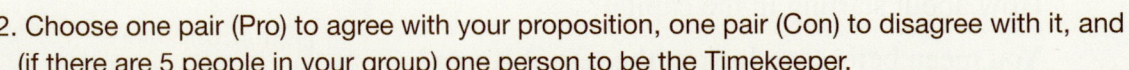

2. Choose one pair (Pro) to agree with your proposition, one pair (Con) to disagree with it, and (if there are 5 people in your group) one person to be the Timekeeper.

Pro/Con Pair, Speaker 1:
▶ These phrases will help you present your arguments:

Right?	Okay so far?	Let me give you an example.
You understand?	Have you got it?	To illustrate my point, …
Got me?	Know what I mean?	Please let me finish.
Got it?	For example, …	I haven't finished yet.
Are you following me?	For instance, …	I'm almost done.
Are you with me?	Take for example …	Hold on a second.

Pro/Con Pair, Speaker 2
▶ These phrases will help you to question the previous speaker:

Really?	Are you serious?	To get back to the point …
Is that right?	Go ahead.	To return to …
Are you sure?	You first.	In any case, …
How do you know?	I can wait.	Where was I?
Who told you that?	Never mind.	What were we talking about?
No way!	Anyway,	May I say something?

Timekeeper: These phrases will help you control the debate.

Today's proposition is …	Speaking for the proposition is ….
You have two minutes to speak.	Speaking against the proposition is ….
Your time is up.	The next speaker is …
Next speaker please.	The proposition has been accepted.
Your conclusions please.	The proposition has been rejected.

Let's Debate!

① **Pro Pair:** Look at pages 62, 70, 86 and 102 for debate language and phrases.
Then write three reasons for agreeing with the proposition, plus your conclusion.

② **Con Pair:** Look at pages 62, 70, 86 and 102 for debate language and phrases.
Then write three reasons for disagreeing with the proposition, plus your conclusion.

③ **Timekeeper:** Look at page 102 and think how you will start and end the debate.

First of all, ...
_____
_____
_____

Next, ...
_____
_____
_____

Furthermore, ...
_____
_____
_____

In conclusion, ...
_____
_____
_____

There are some sample arguments on the next page.

Let's Begin! Us Groups

Timekeeper:

1. Start the debate (see page 102).

2. Ask the first Pro speaker to state the 'Pro' arguments.
   Tell him/her that he/she has 2 minutes.

3. Ask the first Con speaker to state the 'Con' arguments.
   Tell him/her that he/she has 2 minutes.

4. Ask the second Pro student to speak and give his/her conclusions.
   Tell him/her that he/she has 2 minutes.

5. Ask the second Con student to speak and give his/her conclusions.
   Tell him/her that he/she has 2 minutes.

6. End the debate. Either you can decide which team had the best arguments, or you can ask another group to decide. If there is an audience, you can put the proposition to the vote.

Argument Samples Us Groups

- Here are two samples to give you some ideas (Tracks 43 and 44).
- They are about the proposition "Koreans should explore Korea before traveling abroad".
- Can you find phrases from page 102 in these samples?

Pro Speaker 1: I am in favor of the proposition. It's important for me to know about my homeland. I think many people take it for granted. Know what I mean? They don't explore Korea and see how wonderful it is. Are you with me? To illustrate my point, how many countries have such beautiful cherry-blossom festivals? Where else can you visit famous temples and experience the culture of the ancients? I'm almost done. With all these wonderful attractions on my doorstep, I don't need to go abroad. Right?

Con Speaker 1: I agree that Korea has a lot to offer, but I also want to travel overseas and experience other cultures. Okay so far? I'd like to see how other people live and go to places that I've only seen in books. For example, it would be great to visit Europe and take in famous places. Take for example the Eiffel Tower in Paris and Buckingham Palace in London. There would be so much to do, and so many sights to see. Then, when I returned, I'd be able to appreciate Korea much more.

Reflection Me

- How are your learning skills now?
- There are no correct answers. Just write about yourself.

My Learning Skills	
Goal-setting	
Planning	
Organizing	
Study skills	
Reflecting	

There are more puzzles and other activities on the website at www.inkbooks.co.kr

13 Myths

Brainstorming

- Myths and legends are ancient stories about gods, ancestors, or heroes.
- Do you know any myths? Have you heard of Greek myths?

Task 1

- Read this Greek myth called 'Pandora's Box.'
- Can you find sentence number 1? Look for the oval. ①
- Which is the next sentence? Write '2' in the oval next to the sentence.
- Complete the myth together, using all the sentences (1 to 10).

○ He told her never to open it, and gave the key to her husband.

Pandora was very curious about the box. ○

○ One day he fell asleep, and she stole the key.

○ Pandora tried to catch them, but it was too late.

Pandora sat and cried. Then the last thing flew out. ○

○ The last thing was hope. ① Pandora was a beautiful woman.

She asked her husband to open it, but he always said "No." ○

○ She opened the box and all the troubles of the world flew out.

The King of the Gods gave her a little box. ○

*The answers are in the Answer Key, at the back of the book.

Task 2

- Make a mini-drama based on this Greek myth.
- Perform your mini-drama to other students.

Student A: You are Pandora.
Student B: You are the King of the Gods.
Student C: You are Pandora's husband.

Creation Myths

- Listen to Track 45 on the CD-Rom.
- Read these myths about the beginning of human life.
- Check(✓) the name of the people who made each myth.

 Groups

A tiger and a bear both lived in a cave. They wanted to become human, so they prayed to Hwanung, who gave them 20 cloves of garlic and some mugwort. There were two conditions: i) They should eat only this food; ii) They should stay out of the sunlight for 100 days. The tiger gave up after twenty days. The bear remained for 100 days and was changed into a woman.
☐ Australian Aborigines ☐ Ethiopians ☐ Koreans ☐ American Indians

In the beginning, the Father of All Spirits woke the Sun Mother, saying "Go and wake the spirits on the earth." The Sun Mother went, and as she walked on the earth, plants grew. Then she went into the dark mountain caves. Her light woke the insects and her heat melted the ice, creating rivers and streams. Then she woke the birds and animals. Finally, she gave birth to two children, who became our ancestors.
☐ Australian Aborigines ☐ Ethiopians ☐ Koreans ☐ American Indians

The woman and the man dreamed that they were in God's dream. They saw a great, shining egg, so they sang and danced inside the egg. They were crazy with desire to be born, so God, still dreaming, created them. As he did so, he sang: "I break this egg. The woman is born and the man is born. Together they will live and die. They will always be born, die, and be born again between the Atlantic and the Pacific."
☐ Australian Aborigines ☐ Ethiopians ☐ Koreans ☐ American Indians

Wak, the creator God, lived in the clouds. He told man to make a coffin. Then he buried man in the coffin for seven years. During that time it rained fire and the mountains were made. Wak dug up the coffin and man jumped out. Wak took some of his blood and made a woman. They married and had 30 children, but the man was ashamed, so he hid 15 of them. They became African animals and spirits.
☐ Australian Aborigines ☐ Ethiopians ☐ Koreans ☐ American Indians

*The answers are in the Answer Key, at the back of the book.

Match the words and phrases on the left to the definitions on the right.

cloves	a box for holding a dead person
mugwort	a green herb used in medicine and tea
condition	a rule; restriction; limit
crazy with desire	fire came out of the sky like rain; volcanoes
coffin	guilty; regretful; embarrassed
rained fire	really wanting to do something; almost mad
ashamed	small buds or bulbs

There are more reading passages at www.inkbooks.co.kr

Comprehension Check

1. Why did the bear and the tiger pray to Hwanung?
2. What did they have to do in order to become human?
3. Did they both succeed?
4. Why did the Sun Mother visit the earth?
5. What happened when she went to the caves?
6. Where was the shining egg?
7. Was God awake when he created man and woman?
8. What is the name of the Ethiopian God?
9. How did the creator God make a woman?

Think for Yourself

- [ ] Do you know any myths about gods, ancestors, or heroes?
- [ ] Have you heard of Norse Mythology?
- [ ] Have you heard of the 1001 Tales of the Arabian Nights?
- [ ] Have you heard of Grimm's Fairy Tales?
- [ ] Do you know any Korean folktales?
- [ ] How is a myth different from a fairy story or a folktale?

Background Information

Have you heard of these Greek (and Roman) Gods?

- [ ] Aphrodite (Venus) was the goddess of love and beauty.
- [ ] Apollo was the god of music and healing.
- [ ] Ares (Mars) was the god of war.
- [ ] Artemis (Diana) was the goddess of animals.
- [ ] Athena (Minerva) was the goddess of arts and crafts.
- [ ] Eros (Cupid) was the god of love and desire.
- [ ] Dionysus (Bacchus) was the god of wine.
- [ ] Hades (Pluto) was the god of the underworld.
- [ ] Hera (Juno) was the queen of the gods.
- [ ] Hermes (Mercury) was the messenger of the gods.
- [ ] Poseidon (Neptune) was the god of the sea.
- [ ] Zeus (Jupiter, Jove) was the king of the gods.

Discussion Us Groups

- Talk about the questions below.
- Use the Conversation Strategies at the bottom of the page.

1 What is your favorite Korean myth?
  ▶ Tell your favorite myths to each other.

2 Do you know any myths from other countries?
  ▶ Explain the myths to each other.

3 Do you know any ghost stories?
  ▶ Explain the stories to each other.

4 Can you think of any modern mythical characters? (Superman, Spiderman, etc.)
  ▶ Why do people like reading about these characters?

5 Do you have a favorite mythical character?
  ▶ Is he/she ancient or modern?
  ▶ Do you want to be like him/her?

6 Do different cultures have similar myths?
  ▶ Why do you think this is?

7 Are myths just stories, or do they tell us about life?
  ▶ Support your opinion.

8 Do we still need myths, now that we have science and the Internet?
  ▶ What do you think? Why?

Conversation Strategies

Putting events in sequenc:	Adding information:
First of all,	In addition,
In the first place,	Additionally,
Second(ly),	Furthermore
Third(ly),	Moreover
Next,	As well,
After that,	Besides,
Lastly,	Not to mention …
Finally,	What's more, …

Dialogue

- Listen to Track 46 on the CD-Rom.
- Read the dialogue with your partner.
- Perform the dialogue together.
- Change roles. Perform the dialogue again.

Kevin	Hi, Grandma.
Grandma	Hi, Kevin. What are you watching?
Kevin	It's an animation about a youth and his lover.
Grandma	Sounds interesting. What happens?
Kevin	He fights the enemy to get a magic flute back, and he's almost killed, when …
Seung-min	*(Looking up from his homework)* Don't tell me. His lover gives up her life to become a flying horse and rescues the magic flute from the enemy.
Kevin	That's right, Seung-min. How did you know?
Grandma	Yes, spill the beans, Seung-min.
Seung-min	I learned it in Korea before I came to the US. It is called "Hwarang Giparang."
Grandma	And what happens next?
Seung-min	Giparang dies and becomes a flying horse, to be with his lover again.
Kevin	Is that the end? Do they live happily ever after?
Seung-min	In a way. The story ends with them living for ever and protecting Korea.
Grandma	That's a beautiful myth. Do you have any more for us?
Kevin	Maybe another time, Grandma, Seung-min's got homework to finish.

Key Words and Expressions

youth
young person

"Don't tell me."
"I know what you're going to say."

"Spill the beans."
"Share your knowledge (or secret) with us."

Hwarang
"Flower Nights," Young Korean noblemen in the 10th century

happily ever after
Many myths and movies end with the lovers living "happily ever after".

Dialogue Quiz

1. Do you know this story?
   - Do you know the name of Giparang's lover?*
   - Why is the magic flute important?
2. What is Seung-min doing while Kevin is watching the animation?
3. How does Seung-min know the story?
4. What does Grandma want Seung-min to do?

*The answer is in the Answer Key, at the back of the book.

Action Stories Us Groups

- Choose someone to be the Speaker.
- Other people: Stand up and do the actions.
- Speaker: Read the text in the box on the left.

Speaker (Reading)

"There was once a great big …"
"tall …"
"old …"
"tree …"
"which lived near a river …,"
"with tall grass…"
"which blew in the wind."
"There was also a little child,"
"who loved the tree"
"and used to climb in its branches."
"One day the wind blew."
"It blew and it blew."
"And it blew the tree down."
"And men came to chop up the tree."
"So when the child came to visit,"
"The tree had gone."

Others (Actions)

- Stretch your arms wide.
- Strech your arms high.
- Walk like an old person.
- Stick your arms out like a tree.
- Move your hands like river waves.
- Raise your hands above your head.
- Bend to the left and the right.
- Crouch on your heels.
- Hug each other.
- Make climbing movements.
- Walk into the wind. Bend forward.
- Turn round and around.
- Fall down on the ground.
- Swing your arms up and down.
- Walk around.
- Search for the tree.

- Choose someone to be the Speaker.
- Other people: Stand up and do the actions.
- Speaker: Read the text in the box on the left.

Storyteller

1. "A man was lost in a forest."
2. "It got dark."
3. "Then it got cold."
4. "Then it rained."
5. "Then the wind blew strongly."
6. "Then he fell and broke his arm."
7. "A tree fell on him, breaking his legs."
8. "Then he heard wolves coming."
9. "Finally, he awoke. He had been dreaming."

Others (Actions)

1. Walk around. Look. Search.
2. You can't see anything.
   Search even harder. Listen.
3. Be cold! Use all your body.
4. Be wet! Hide from the rain.
   Use your coat as an umbrella.
5. Fight against the wind. Be cold and wet!
6. Fall over. Hold your arm. It's painful!
7. Hold your legs. It really hurts. Scream!
8. Listen. Oh no! Use all your body.
9. Wake up. Be surprised. Be happy!

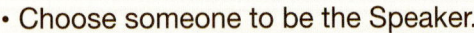

Let's Make a Story! 

Task 1: Chain Story 1

- You are going to make an action story together.
- When you make a sentence, you must repeat what the people before you said and do the actions.
- Then you add your action and perform it.

1. **Student 1**: "When I go home I will ………."
2. **Student 2**: "When I go home I will ………. and …………"
3. **Student 3**: "When I go home I will ………. and ………… and …………."
4. **Student 4**: "When I go home I will ………. and ………… and ………….. and …………."
5. Continue. Each student adds a new action until the story finishes.

Task 2: Chain Story 2

- You are going to make another story together. It can be about anything at all.
- You must add a sentence when it is your turn.
- Use the conversation strategies on page 108.
- Keep going! How many sentences can you remember?

Here is an example:

Student 1: Once upon a time there was a man.
Student 2: Once upon a time there was a man. He was driving to work.
Student 3: Once upon a time there was a man. He was driving to work. Then he saw a house on fire.
Student 4: Once upon a time there was a man. He was driving to work. Then he saw a house on fire. So he got out of his car.
Next student: Once upon a time there was a man. He was driving to work. Then he saw a house on fire. So he got out of his car. ……………………………………………………………………………………

Task 3: Chain Story 3

- Make another story together. It can be about anything at all.
- You must add a sentence when it is your turn.
- But you don't have to repeat the other sentences.
- Use the conversation strategies on page 108.
- Be creative!

Unit 13 Myths

My Speaking Skills

- How were your speaking skills when you had a discussion (page 108)?
- How were they when you made some stories (page 111)?
- Assess your English speaking skills in the table below.

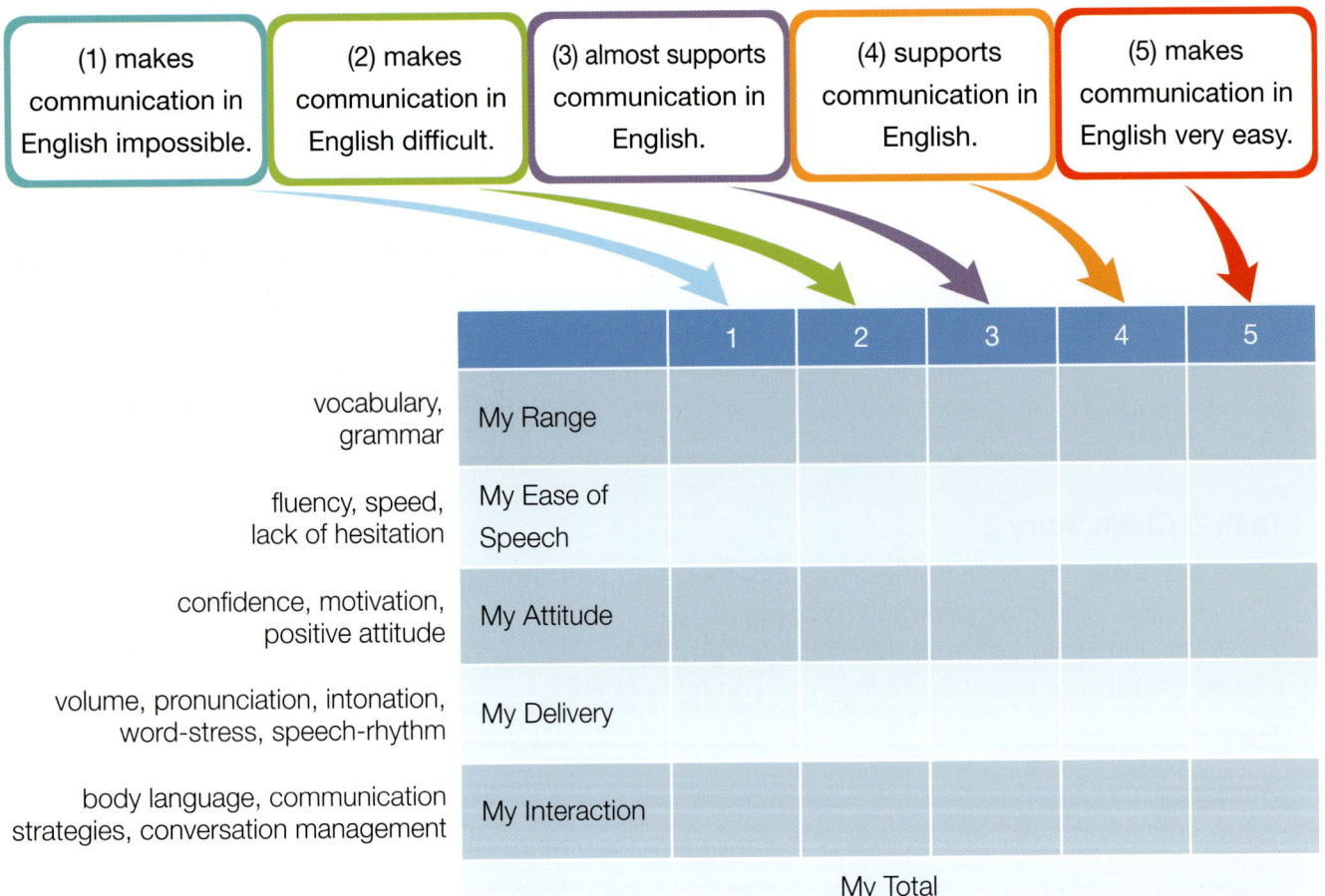

		1	2	3	4	5
vocabulary, grammar	My Range					
fluency, speed, lack of hesitation	My Ease of Speech					
confidence, motivation, positive attitude	My Attitude					
volume, pronunciation, intonation, word-stress, speech-rhythm	My Delivery					
body language, communication strategies, conversation management	My Interaction					
	My Total					

(1) makes communication in English impossible.
(2) makes communication in English difficult.
(3) almost supports communication in English.
(4) supports communication in English.
(5) makes communication in English very easy.

Review

- Now review what you have done in this Unit and prepare for the next Unit.

Review — Browse the website for Unit 13.

Preview — Browse the website for Unit 14.

Prepare — Look at the activities in Unit 14.

There are more puzzles and other activities on the website at www.inkbooks.co.kr

14 Smart Technology

Brainstorming

- Do you have a cell phone?
- How long have you had it?
- How often do you use it?
- Could you live without it?

Task 1

- Sit with your back to your partner.
- Choose a situation (below) and have a conversation together.
- Imagine you are phoning each other (you can use your phones).
- Perform your conversation to other people.
- Can you make your own cell phone situation?

A: You bought a sweater yesterday for your mother's birthday, but she didn't like it. Ring the department store. Ask for your money back.

B: You are the shop assistant. The department store does not give refunds. However, the customer can choose another sweater.

A: You want to go to the beach for the weekend. Make a booking at a hotel. Explain what sort of room you want, how many nights, etc.

B: You are the hotel receptionist. Ask A "How many nights?" "What sort of room?" "How will you pay? Cash or credit card?"

A: Your parents' wedding anniversary is tomorrow. Ring the flower shop. Say what sort of flowers you want, ask the price and give the delivery address.

B: You are the flower shop assistant. Ask what sort of flowers A wants (how many, what color, what type, etc.). Explain the price and ask for the delivery address.

A: You have just seen two cars crash into each other. Phone the police and ask them to come quickly. Tell them what happened.

B: You are a police officer. Tell Student A that you will send someone as soon as possible. Ask A to tell you what happened.

Smart phones

- Listen to Track 47 on the CD-Rom.
- Read this passage together.
- While you read, match the words and phrases at the bottom of the page.
- Then answer the questions on the next page.

 Groups

Have you seen people talking on their cell phones on the bus or in the subway? Isn't it strange how they talk so loudly, letting everyone know what they are talking about? Or how about the couples in restaurants talking to their cell phones instead of to each other? Everywhere we go, we can see people texting, emailing, playing games, reading online newspapers, surfing the Internet, or taking photos. It's no exaggeration to say that mobile phones have revolutionized our lives.

The number of cell phone users worldwide in 2006 was 2.6 billion. This had risen to 4.6 billion by 2016, due to new subscribers in Africa, the Middle East and India. Wireless communication is particularly good for developing countries, since they don't have to set up telephone lines across the country. Now, people who have never heard a dial tone in their lives can use a cordless phone to speak to anyone, anytime, anywhere.

There have been many generations of cell phones since a Motorola researcher made the first mobile telephone call in 1973. More than 40 years later, they have become multifunctional devices with access to the Internet, messaging, cameras, games, maps, apps, and many other features. But what will they look like in 10 or 20 years time?

Researchers say that the phones of the future will have higher definition and faster Internet speed, but that's not all! They're talking about concept phones (many shapes and forms) and phones with speed and heat detectors and other super-high-tech features. Instead of being just a tool for communication, our phones will be telling us about the nearest restaurant or cinema, the best route home, and even our health. It certainly makes you think!

Match the words and phrases on the left to the definitions on the right.

Word/Phrase	Definition
exaggeration	a device that can tell if something is present
revolutionize	a statement claiming that something is bigger than it is
subscribers	countries that are not yet industrialized
wireless	food for thought (page 58); something to think about
developing countries	having many uses
set up	not using any wires or cables
dial tone	people who own cell phones
multifunctional	the noise heard before dialing a number on a telephone
detector	install; lay down; make
It makes you think.	to change completely; cause a revolution

There are more reading passages at www.inkbooks.co.kr

Comprehension Check

1. Can you find two other terms for "cell phone" in the passage?
2. When was the first mobile phone call?
3. How many subscribers were there in 2006 and 2016?
4. Why are cell phones good for developing countries?
5. What is a concept phone?
6. How will heat detectors help phone owners?

Think for Yourself

- [ ] What do you use your cell phone for?
    - How many text messages do you send each day?
    - Do you use it for educational purposes?
- [ ] If you could make your own cell phone:
    - What would it look like?
    - What would you be able to do with it?

Background Information

Did you know?

- [ ] There were only 4.3 million cell phone subscribers in 1990.
- [ ] 130 million cell phones are thrown away each year.
- [ ] Up to 60% of the radiation from a typical cell phone goes into the user's head.
- [ ] Millions of birds die each year in the US because of flying into cell phone towers.
- [ ] Cell phone radiation makes it hard for bees to find their home. In a recent study, 70% of bees did not return to hives containing cell phones.
- [ ] In Santiago City, in the Philippines, mobile phones are banned in public places.
- [ ] Julia Roberts does not own a TV. She has a mobile phone, but rarely switches it on.
- [ ] 33% of subscribers say their phones are for emergencies only.
- [ ] Scientists say that the size of cell phones becomes 50% smaller every 18 months.
- [ ] 58% of Norwegian businessmen think it is rude to use a mobile phone in a supermarket.

Discussion *Groups*

- Talk together about the questions below.
- Use the Conversation Strategies at the bottom of the page.

1. **Is it OK to use cell phones in public places?**
   - Why? Why not? Support your opinion.
2. **What do you use your cell phone for?**
   - How many uses can you think of?
3. **Could you live without your cellphone?**
   - What did people do before telephones?
4. **Do you have a SNS, Facebook or Twitter account?**
   - Why? Why not?
5. **What are the advantages and disadvantages of smart phones?**
   - Explain your opinion.
6. **What is the greatest technological invention?**
   - Explain your opinion.
7. **What can robots do better than humans?**
   - Will robots cause unemployment?
   - What do you think about artificial intelligence (AI)?
   - Can robots think?
8. **Are you a Mac or PC user?**
   - What are the differences?
9. **Would you buy a self-driving car?**
   - Why? Why not? Explain your opinion.
10. **Does smart technology reduce or increase stress?**
    - Explain your opinion.

Conversation Strategies

Sharing news on the phone:	Receiving news on the phone:
Have you heard …?	Really?
They say that …	Is that so?
I've heard that ….	Are you sure?
Don't tell anyone, but …	You're kidding!
A little bird told me …..	Are you serious?
Between you and me …	Do you really mean that?

Dialogue

- Listen to Track 48 on the CD-Rom.
- Read the dialogue with your partners.
- Perform the dialogue together.
- Change roles. Perform the dialogue again.

Track 48

(Jenny's cell phone rings.)

Jenny	Hi, Jenny here.
Mr. Brown	Ah, hello Jenny. How's the shopping?
Jenny	Oh, hi, dad. It's going well. I've nearly finished.
Mr. Brown	How long do you need?
Jenny	About 30 minutes or so.
Mr. Brown	How about meeting at the Soft Rock Café in an hour?
Jenny	That sounds like a plan. Then we can go home together.
Mr. Brown	OK. I'll park the car and meet you there.

(An hour later, at the Soft Rock Café. Mr. Brown's cell phone rings.)

Mr. Brown	Hello. Is that you, Jenny?
Jenny	Yes, dad. Where are you? I've been waiting for ages.
Mr. Brown	What do you mean? I'm waiting for you.
Jenny	But I'm in the Café and I can't see you.
Mr. Brown	I'm in the Café, and I can't see you!

(Jenny and Mr. Brown turn round. They were sitting back to back.)

Jenny and Mr. Brown	Ah! There you are!

Key Words and Expressions

"Jenny here."
"This is Jenny."
"Jenny speaking."

"How long do you need?"
"When will you finish?"

… or so
about; approximately

"That sounds like a plan."
"That's a good idea."

for ages
for a very long time

Dialogue Quiz

1. Why does Mr. Brown ring Jenny?
2. What is Jenny doing?
3. What do they agree to do?
4. Why does Jenny ring Mr. Brown?
5. Who is in the wrong place?
6. Why couldn't they see each other?
7. Do we rely on our phones too much?

Debate Corner

1. In your group (4 or 5 people), choose one of the propositions below.

- Smart phones are making us stupid.
- Computers will soon be smarter than humans.
- Technology is causing many problems today.
- Human cloning should be banned.

2. Choose one pair (Pro) to agree with your proposition, one pair (Con) to disagree with it, and (if there are 5 people in your group) one person to be the Timekeeper.

Pro/Con Pair, Speaker 1:
▶ These phrases will help you present your arguments.

Do you believe that …?	What do you think of …?	The best way is …
Do you think we should …?	There are exceptions.	We really have to …
Would you consider …?	This does include …	Alternatively, …
Are you for or against …?	Except, of course …	Instead, …
Would you prefer …?	One exception is …	On the other hand, …
Would you rather …?	The solution is …	There again, …

Pro/Con Pair, Speaker 2
▶ These phrases will help you to question the previous speaker.

Don't they …?	Why shouldn't they?	In that case,
Don't you think that …?	What if …?	In that respect,
Don't you see that …?	What happens if …?	As far as that goes …
Can't you see that …?	If that is so …,	On that point, …
Wouldn't it be better to …?	You would be right if …	You lost me there.
Wouldn't you agree that …?	That would make sense if …	I'm not following.

Timekeeper: These phrases will help you control the debate.

Today's proposition is …	Speaking for the proposition is ….
You have two minutes to speak.	Speaking against the proposition is ….
Your time is up.	The next speaker is …
Next speaker please.	The proposition has been accepted.
Your conclusions please.	The proposition has been rejected.

Let's Debate!

❶ Pro Pair: Look at pages 62, 70, 86, 102 and 118 for debate language and phrases. Then write three reasons for agreeing with the proposition, plus your conclusion.

❷ Con Pair: Look at pages 62, 70, 86, 102 and 118 for debate language and phrases. Then write three reasons for disagreeing with the proposition, plus your conclusion.

❸ Timekeeper: Look at page 118 and think of how you will start and end the debate.

First of all, ...	Next, ...
_____	_____
_____	_____
_____	_____

Furthermore, ...	In conclusion, ...
_____	_____
_____	_____
_____	_____

There are some sample arguments on the next page.

Let's Begin! Us Groups

Timekeeper:

1. Start the debate (see page 118).

2. Ask the first Pro speaker to state the 'Pro' arguments.
   Tell him/her that he/she has 2 minutes.

3. Ask the first Con speaker to state the 'Con' arguments.
   Tell him/her that he/she has 2 minutes.

4. Ask the second Pro student to speak and give his/her conclusions.
   Tell him/her that he/she has 2 minutes.

5. Ask the second Con student to speak and give his/her conclusions.
   Tell him/her that he/she has 2 minutes.

6. End the debate. Either you can decide which team had the best arguments, or you can ask another group to decide. If there is an audience, you can put the proposition to the vote.

Argument Samples Us ▶ Groups

- Here are two samples to give you some ideas (Tracks 49 and 50).
- They are about the proposition "Smart phones are making us stupid".
- Can you find phrases from page 118 in these samples?

Pro Speaker 1: Would you consider going a day without your smartphone? Would you prefer to be glued to the screen all day? Do you believe that smartphones are taking over our lives? Some people are even addicted to their phone. They can't do anything without checking it or sending texts. There are exceptions of course, but many people now rely on their phones for everything: information, maps, calculation, you name it. People just aren't thinking any more. They let their phones do everything for them.

Con Speaker 1: Don't you think that the previous speaker has got things wrong? Wouldn't you agree that smartphones have helped us to become even more intelligent? We can find any information we want and discuss our findings with friends in real time. We can also find people with the same interests and spend our free time watching videos and listening to music. What if we stop using smartphones? Would it make us smarter? I don't think so. As far as that goes, the other speaker lost me there.

Reflection Me

- How are your social skills now?
- There are no correct answers. Just write about yourself.

My Social Skills	
Team work	
Consideration	
Leadership	
Body language	
Positive attitude	

There are more reading passages at www.inkbooks.co.kr

15 Water

Brainstorming
- How much water do you use each day?
- Where does our water come from?
- Where does it go after we have used it?

Task 1
Water Survey

Student A: Ask these questions to five people.

	❶	❷	❸	❹	❺
How many times do you wash your face each day?					
How many times do you brush your teeth each day?					
How many times do you flush the toilet each day?					
How many times do you take a shower each day?					

Student B: Ask these questions to five people.

	❶	❷	❸	❹	❺
Do you let the water run when you brush your teeth?					
Do you let the water run when you wash your face?					
Do you try to save water when you have a shower?					
Do you ever forget to turn the water off?					

Task 2
Data Analysis
- Make some sentences to describe your results.
- For example: Some people try to save water when they have a shower.

Everybody	
Most people	
Some people	
Almost nobody	
Nobody	

Unit 15 Water 121

Water Shortage

- Listen to Track 51 on the CD-Rom.
- Read this passage together.
- While you read, match the words and phrases at the bottom of the page.
- Then answer the questions on the next page

 Groups

It's easy to think that water shortage is a Third World problem. However, the World Wildlife Fund has warned that even developed countries face water shortages, due to climate change and bad water management. Economic wealth does not mean an endless supply of water anymore, and even cities such as Houston and Sydney have to cut back. As for the UK, the WWF report says that London loses 300 Olympic swimming pools of water every day because of old, leaking water pipes.

Believe it or not, the water we use now is the same water that was on the earth millions of years ago. However, we are using it at an ever-increasing rate, and rivers and lakes are drying up as the water table continues to drop. Not only have 815 lakes disappeared from China's Thousand-Lake Province (Hubei), but glaciers are getting smaller in Europe and Greenland, because of global warming. South Africa has experienced its worst drought in living memory, Australia has reported its worst drought in 1000 years, and California's 4 years without rain have not been equalled in 1200 years. It has even been suggested that wars will be fought for water in the future.

Seventy percent of the world's surface is covered by water, but we can only use about 0.3% of this, from groundwater, rivers, and freshwater lakes. The WWF is therefore asking for global cooperation and in 1993 the United Nations declared March 22 to be World Water Day. Wealthy countries must act first to maintain water supplies by replacing aging water systems and fighting water pollution.

Match the words and phrases on the left to the definitions on the right.

Third World	a large mass of snow and ice
developed countries	a long period without rain
cut back	countries round the world helping each other
Believe it or not,	countries that are already rich and industrialized
water table	increase in the earth's temperature
glacier	keep in good condition, look after
drought	the level below which the ground contains water
global warming	under-developed countries
groundwater	use less and less
global cooperation	water beneath the earth's surface
maintain	you might find this hard to believe, but …

Comprehension Check

1. What does 'WWF' mean?
2. Is the water shortage only in under-developed countries?
3. What has caused the water shortage?
4. Do developed countries have plenty of water?
5. Why is so much water wasted in London?
6. Give an example of the over-use of water.
7. Why could wars be fought over water?
8. Where does our drinking water come from?
9. When is World Water Day?

Think for Yourself

- [ ] What are the causes of global warming?
- [ ] How does it affect our water supply?
- [ ] How can we save water?

Background Information

Did you know?

- [ ] The average American uses 300 - 375 liters of water per day.
- [ ] Americans use 408 billion gallons of water per day.
- [ ] Many people in the world use less than 10 liters of water a day. This is almost the same as one flush of the toilet.
- [ ] A dripping faucet wastes up to four liters of water a day.
- [ ] About one third of the water in the UK is lost through leaking pipes before it gets to people's homes.
- [ ] 97% of earth's water is in the oceans.
- [ ] The polar ice caps contain 75% of the world's fresh water.
- [ ] The record for living without food is about 70 days. We cannot live without water for more than one week.
- [ ] 4 of every 10 people in the world face a daily water shortage.
- [ ] An average water molecule spends 98 years in the ocean, 20 months as ice, about 2 weeks in lakes and rivers, and less than a week in the atmosphere.
- [ ] Water is the only substance that is found naturally on earth in three forms: liquid, gas, and solid.

Discussion Us Groups

- Talk about the questions below.
- Use the Conversation Strategies at the bottom of the page.

1. **Do you buy bottled water or drink tap water?**
   - ▶ Why? Explain your preference.

2. **What would you do if you had no running water?**

3. **What things do you do each day that require water?**
   - ▶ How much water do you need each day?

4. **Is access to water a human right?**
   - ▶ Why? Why not? Explain your opinion.

5. **Do you think water should be free?**
   - ▶ Why? Why not? Explain your opinion.

6. **"We never know the worth of water till the well is dry."** (Thomas Fuller, 1732)
   - ▶ Do you agree? Why? Why not?

7. **"Water and air (…) have become global garbage cans."** (Jacques Cousteau)
   - ▶ Do you agree? Why? Why not?

8. **"The frog does not drink up the pond in which he lives."** (American Indian proverb)
   - ▶ What does this mean?
   - ▶ Do you know any similar proverbs?

9. **What can be done to save water?**
   - ▶ What should the government do?
   - ▶ What should companies do?
   - ▶ What should we do? (See page 128.)

He's abusing water.

Conversation Strategies

Sharing surprising information:

| Believe it or not, |
| Surprisingly enough, |
| Oddly enough, |
| Strangely enough, |
| You might not believe it, but … |

Generalizing:

| On the whole, |
| By and large, |
| Generally, |
| As a rule, |
| Usually, |

Dialogue

- Lsten to Track 52 on the CD-Rom.
- Read the dialogue with your partner.
- Perform the dialogue together.
- Change roles. Perform the dialogue again.

Track 52

Ji-hye	Hello, Jenny.
Jenny	Hi, Ji-hye. Guess what?
Ji-hye	What is it? I'm all ears.
Jenny	Did you know it's World Water Day tomorrow?
Ji-hye	Really? That's news to me.
Jenny	It's true. I just read it in a magazine.
Ji-hye	Why don't we do something to save water?
Jenny	That's just what I was thinking. But what can we do?
Ji-hye	I know … Let's fix that leaking faucet in the bathroom.
Jenny	That's a good idea.
Ji-hye	And how about taking a really short shower?
Jenny	OK. Let's make a list of things we can do.
Ji-hye	Yes, and then we can show it to everyone else.
Jenny	We can be a water-saving family!
Ji-hye	I agree. Let's do it.

Key Words and Expressions

"Guess what?"
"I have something interesting to tell you."

"I'm all ears."
"I'm ready to hear what you have to say"

"That's news to me."
"I didn't know that."

"I know."
"I have an idea."

Dialogue Quiz

1. What is the date in this dialogue? (Look at reading passage, page 122.)
2. How did Jenny find out about World Water Day?
3. Did Ji-hye already know about it?
4. What do they decide to do?
5. How do they decide to save water?
6. What will they do after this dialogue?

Let's Make a Courtroom Drama! Us Groups

In Units 1 to 14 we made role-plays and debates. Now we're going to combine these and make a mock trial.

- Look at the situation on this page and make a courtroom drama.
- You need a judge, a prosecutor, a witness, a defense lawyer and a company representative.
- Choose your roles and make notes on the next page.
- How about inviting another group to be the jury?

Situation: A chemical company has been storing poisonous chemical waste on its land. This waste has got into the local water supply. Families living nearby are suffering from poisoning, cancer and other diseases.

Prosecuting team:
1. Give the evidence against the company.
2. Interrogate the defense team members.
3. Ask the jury to find the defendants guilty.
4. Ask the judge for the maximum penalty.

- Isn't that correct?
- Let me call your attention to …
- Do you recall making this statement?
- I remind you that you are still under oath.
- I'll rephrase the question.
- I have no further questions.
- The evidence is overwhelming.
- The defendant acted knowingly.
- At this time the government rests.

- If it pleases the court…
- I call as my first witness …
- Isn't it a fact that … ?

Defending team:
1. Answer the prosecutor's questions.
2. Give your side of the argument.
3. Provide your own evidence.
4. Plead not guilty.

- We followed the waste laws.
- I object on the grounds that …
- You cannot prove that ….
- That is not true.
- The defendant is innocent until proven guilty.
- The defendant says he is sorry and remorseful.
- At this time the defense rests.

- My company denies everything.

Judge:
1. Control the courtroom procedure.
2. Use judicial language.
3. Ask the jury to give their decision.

- How do you plead?
- Rephrase the question.
- Please proceed.
- You may cross-examine, counsel.
- Will the defendant please rise.
- You can resume your seat.
- You may step down.
- Have you reached a verdict?
- The defendant is guilty as charged.
- Do you have anything to say?

- Call your next witness.
- State your full name.
- Do you swear to tell the truth, the whole truth and nothing but the truth?

The Trial! Groups

- Prosecutor and witness: Write three things that you want to talk about.
- Lawyer and defendant: Write three things that you want to say.
- Judge: Look at the trial structure on this page.

Opening statement
___
___
___

Evidence
___
___
___

Questions
___
___
___

Conclusion
___
___
___

Let's Begin!

Judge:

1. Swear in the jury.
2. Ask the prosecutor to make an opening statement.
   Tell him/her that he/she has 2 minutes.
3. Ask the defending lawyer to make an opening statement.
   Tell him/her that he/she has 2 minutes.
4. Swear in the witness ("Do you swear that … and nothing but the truth?").
5. Let the prosecutor examine the witness.
6. Let the defence lawyer cross-examine the witness.
7. Swear in the defendant ("Do you swear that … and nothing but the truth?").
8. Examine the defendant (defense lawyer and then prosecutor).
9. Ask for closing arguments (prosecutor and then defending lawyer).
10. Ask the jury to announces its decision (verdict).
11. Give the sentence (if the defendant is found guilty).

Unit 15 Water 127

Tips for saving water

1. Take shorter showers.
2. Don't let the water run while washing your face or brushing your teeth.
3. Use washing machines only when they are fully loaded.
4. When washing dishes, fill the sink with water. Don't run the water all the time. Quickly rinse the dishes at the end.
5. Try to do one thing each day to save water.
6. Tell your friends to "Turn it Off," and "Keep it Off."
7. Every drop counts. Everyone can make a difference.
8. Never put water down the drain when you can use it for watering a plant or cleaning.

Puzzle: The Seven Bridges of Königsberg

Königsberg (now Kaliningrad, Russia) is a town with seven bridges The citizens used to walk around the town every Sunday, trying to cross each bridge only once. Can you do it? You can start anywhere and finish anywhere, but you must cross every bridge once.

The solution is in the Answer Section at the back of the book.

There are more reading passages at www.inkbooks.co.kr

16 Television

Making a TV Schedule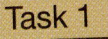

- How often do you watch TV?
- What programs do you watch?
- How many hours do you watch TV each week?

Task 1
- You are going to make a weekend TV schedule together. What do you want to watch?
- Choose the programs and the times and write them below.

Time	Saturday TV

Time	Sunday TV

Task 2
- Show your schedule to another pair of students.
- Talk about your schedule together.

Viewing Habits

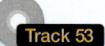

- Listen to Track 53 on the CD-Rom.
- Read this passage together.
- While you read, match the words and phrases at the bottom of the page.
- Then answer the questions on the next page.

 Groups

Did you know that American youths spend on average 900 hours in school and 1500 hours watching television? In other words, watching TV is the most time-consuming thing they do, apart from sleeping. In fact, according to California State University, the average child will see

8,000 murders on TV before finishing elementary school and 200,000 acts of violence by the age of 18. Because of this, the American Psychiatric Association started a National TV-Turnoff Week (now Screen-Free Week) in 1994, saying "We have had a long-standing concern with the impact of television on behavior, especially among children."

Children need to be active in order to develop healthy minds and bodies. Language skills and social skills grow as a result of reading, playing, doing homework and talking with friends and adults. However, children who watch a lot of television tend to: i) have lower school grades; ii) read fewer books; iii) exercise less; and iv) be overweight. Parents therefore need to help their children develop good TV-watching habits. This can be done by:

1. watching programs with their children and asking questions about them;
2. helping their children to choose interesting, non-violent programs;
3. helping their children to analyze commercials;
4. turning the TV off during meals and study time;
5. being a good TV-watching role model.

In conclusion, TV can be a good source of interesting information and entertainment if it's used well. If not, it can harm a child's natural development. If you're interested, how about joining in Screen-Free Week next May, and experiencing an unplugged life for a while? You never know, you might like it!

Match the words and phrases on the left to the definitions on the right.

time-consuming	advance; grow; mature
develop	amusement; pastime; recreation
social skills	consider; evaluate; judge
non-violent	cooperation; teamwork
analyze	not using electricity; disconnected
entertainment	peaceful; without violent scenes
unplugged	taking up time; eating up time

Comprehension Check

1. What is the main pastime of American students?
2. What do children need to do in order to grow in a healthy way?
3. Does television help children to develop healthy minds and bodies?
4. How can you tell if a child watches too much television?
5. How can parents help their children to develop good TV-watching habits?
6. Are the effects of TV all negative?
7. What does the writer suggest at the end of the passage?
8. Why does the writer make this suggestion?

Think for Yourself

- [ ] Do you turn the TV off if you can't find a good show?
- [ ] Do you analyze TV commercials?
- [ ] Have you ever tried not watching the TV for a day?
- [ ] Could you go without watching TV for a month?
- [ ] What are the good effects of television?

Background Information

Did you know?

- [ ] By the time a child reaches age 70, he or she will have watched between 7 and 10 years of television.
- [ ] Watching TV uses only a few more calories than sleeping.
- [ ] 66% of US homes have three or more TV sets.
- [ ] 49% of Americans say they watch too much TV.
- [ ] 79% of Americans think that TV violence encourages violence in real life.
- [ ] Eating junk food and watching television are two major causes of obesity.
- [ ] The average child watches 20,000 thirty-second commercials in a year.
- [ ] Children who watch 5 hours of TV a day are more likely to begin smoking than those who watch less than 2 hours.
- [ ] Children under age 2 should have no "screen time" at all. TV can stop them from growing mentally, physically, socially, and emotionally.

Discussion Us▸Groups

- Talk about the questions below.
- Use the Conversation Strategies at the bottom of the page.

① **What are the good and bad points about television?**
   ▶ Support your opinion.

② **What is your favourite TV commercial?**

③ **Does TV make us lazy?**
   ▶ Support your opinion.

④ **Do you think television harms young children?**
   ▶ Why? Why not? Explain your opinion.

⑤ **Do violent scenes on TV make children violent?**
   ▶ Do they cause violent crimes?

⑥ **What are the good and bad sides of TV news?**
   ▶ Why is there so much crime and violence on TV news?
   ▶ Does TV news give us a true picture of life?

⑦ **Is cable TV better than normal TV?**
   ▶ Why? Why not? Support your opinion.

⑧ **What do you think about TV shopping channels?**
   ▶ Have you ever done any TV shopping?

⑨ **What do you think about reality shows?**

⑩ **Could you live without a TV?**
   ▶ What would you do instead?

Conversation Strategies

Looking ahead:

If I …
If I ever …
When I …
As soon as I …
The moment I …

→ come home, I'll turn on the television.

Routines:

When I …
Whenever I …
As soon as I …
The moment I …
Just after I …

→ come home, I turn on the television.

Dialogue

- Listen to Track 54 on the CD-Rom.
- Read the dialogue with your partner.
- Perform the dialogue together.
- Change roles. Perform the dialogue again.

Key Words and Expressions

soap opera
a drama series based on normal people

obvious
simple; easy; not interesting

one-sided love
love that is not returned; A loves B, but B does not love A.

double-showing
two episodes shown one after the other

(Seung-min is sitting at a table, doing his homework.)

Seung-min   Hi, Jenny.

Jenny   Hey, Seung-min. Do you mind if I turn the TV on?

Seung-min   No, I don't. What's on?

Jenny   It's my favorite soap opera. You know, the one from Korea.

Seung-min   You don't like watching that, do you?

Jenny   What do you mean? It's cool.

Seung-min   But it's so obvious. You can tell what's going to happen. The woman will cry because of one-sided love, and then ….

Jenny   … I know, but I love watching it, anyway.

Seung-min   How about Monday Night Football instead?

Jenny   Oh, come on, Seung-min! Aren't you interested at all?

Seung-min   Well, maybe it's nice to see Seoul and the Korean actors.

Jenny   Thanks. It's only for 25 minutes.

Seung-min   OK, and then I'll get back to my homework.

(one hour later)

Jenny   Sorry, Seung-min. I didn't realize it was a double-showing today. Seung-min?

Seung-min   *(Quietly snoring)* zzzz ………………………….

Dialogue Quiz

1. Does Seung-min get any homework done during this dialogue?
2. Why doesn't Seung-min like the soap opera?
3. Why does he agree to watch it?
4. What would he rather watch?
5. Where does the soap opera take place?
6. How many episodes were shown today?

Debate Corner Groups

1. In your group (4 or 5 people), choose one of the propositions below.

- Television is harmful to young minds.
- There is too much violence on TV.
- Television has a positive influence on society.
- TV commercials should be banned.

2. Choose one pair (Pro) to agree with your proposition, one pair (Con) to disagree with it, and (if there are 5 people in your group) one person to be the Timekeeper.

Pro/Con Pair, Speaker 1:
▶ These phrases help you present and conclude your arguments:

We strongly believe the motion is true.	There are many examples for this.
Let us first define some terms.	You can find many examples.
What do we mean by …. ?	So we can see clearly that …
First of all, I will talk about …	So as we have seen, …
The second speaker will talk about …	Now because of this, ….
My first argument is …	We ask you to support this motion.

Pro/Con Pair, Speaker 2
▶ These phrases help you question the previous speaker and conclude your argument:

Let us look at what … has said.	Wouldn't you agree that … ?
The first speaker has told us that …	I'm going to come to that point.
On the contrary, …	As the first speaker has told you, …
He/she also said that …	I'd like to summarize our argument.
But in fact, …	I beg you to oppose the motion.
We oppose the motion because …	For these reasons the motion must fall.

Timekeeper: These phrases help you control the debate.

Today's motion is …	Speaking for the proposition is ….
You have two minutes to speak.	Speaking against the proposition is ….
Your time is up.	The next speaker is …
Next speaker please.	The proposition has been accepted.
Your conclusions please.	The proposition has been rejected.

Let's Debate!

1. **Pro Pair:** Look at pages 62, 70, 86, 102, 118 and 134 for debate language and phrases. Then write three reasons for agreeing with the motion, plus your conclusion.
2. **Con Pair:** Look at pages 62, 70, 86, 102, 118 and 134 for debate language and phrases. Then write three reasons for disagreeing with the motion, plus your conclusion.
3. **Timekeeper:** Look at page 134 and think of how you will start and end the debate.

First of all, ...
_____
_____
_____

Next, ...
_____
_____
_____

Furthermore, ...
_____
_____
_____

In conclusion, ...
_____
_____
_____

There are some sample arguments on the next page.

Let's Begin! Groups

Timekeeper:

1. Start the debate (see page 134).
2. Ask the first Pro speaker to state the 'Pro' arguments. Tell him/her that he/she has 2 minutes.
3. Ask the first Con speaker to state the 'Con' arguments. Tell him/her that he/she has 2 minutes.
4. Ask the second Pro student to speak and give his/her conclusions. Tell him/her that he/she has 2 minutes.
5. Ask the second Con student to speak and give his/her conclusions. Tell him/her that he/she has 2 minutes.
6. End the debate. Either you can decide which team had the best arguments, or you can ask another group to decide. If there is an audience, you can put the proposition to the vote.

Argument Samples Us Groups

Track 55 and 56

- Here are two samples to give you some ideas (Tracks 55 and 56).
- They are about the proposition "Television has a positive influence on society".
- Can you find phrases from page 134 in these samples?

Pro Speaker 1: My team strongly believes this motion is true. But first let me define "influence". What do we mean by this? According to Merriam-Webster's learner's Dictionary, it means "the power to change or affect something." Therefore we believe that television is able to change our society in a positive way. There are many examples of this. But first I will talk about the history of television, before coming to its current role. Then my partner will talk about the advantages of television for viewers of all ages. Finally, we will sum up and ask you to vote for the motion.

Con Speaker 2: The first speaker has said that television can change society in a positive way. On the contrary, I think TV companies have a lot to answer for. Wouldn't you agree that there's too much violence on TV, even in children's programs? So it's not surprising that people become more violent after watching television. We also oppose the motion because there is no moral education on television. Instead of developing children's minds, TV channels air lots of mindless programs and silly commercials. For these reasons I beg you to vote against the motion.

House Puzzle Us 2

- Can you solve this puzzle together? (The answer is in the Answer Section at the back of the book.)

There are 9 people in a house. Eight people are doing something: ironing, sleeping, dressing, watching TV, playing chess, washing, listening to the radio, or cooking. What is the 9th person doing?

There are more reading passages at www.inkbooks.co.kr

17 Success and Happiness

Picturing the Future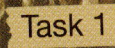
- What is success?
- What is happiness?
- How can we achieve them?

Task 1
- What do you want to achieve in the next 5 years? Where do you want to be?
- Draw two pictures of yourself in 5 years time.

Task 2
- Draw two pictures of yourself in 10 years time.

Task 3
- Talk to your partner about your pictures.
- What does success and happiness mean for you now?
- What will success and happiness mean for you 20 years from now?

Happiness

- Listen to Track 57 on the CD-Rom.
- Read this passage together.
- While you read, match the words and phrases at the bottom of the page.
- Then answer the questions on the next page.

Us Groups

Everyone dreams about success and happiness, but what do these mean in the 21st century? The Greek philosopher, Aristotle, said that the pursuit of happiness is the goal of humanity, and the US Declaration of Independence lists "life, liberty, and the pursuit of happiness" as basic human rights.

Indeed, most of us chase after success and happiness, trying to find them in money, relationships, or possessions. In fact, the answer to our dreams is inside us. All we need to do is believe in ourselves. It sounds too simple to be true, but when you think about it, it makes sense. If you don't believe in yourself, who will?

One way of learning how to do this is called "Affirmation." When you affirm, you remind yourself of your value as a person. This can be done by saying "I believe in myself" or "I can do anything if I do my best" 20 times a day. Another method is called "Visualization." This means imagining yourself as happy and successful. As the American scholar, William Arthur Ward, said, "If you can imagine it, you can achieve it; if you can dream it, you can become it."

Finally, it is a fact of life that positive ideas make positive results and negative ideas make negative results. Just cutting the words "No" and "Can't" from your speech can make a huge difference to your life. Perhaps the song is right when it says "Don't worry, be happy."*

Don't Worry, be Happy was sung by Bobby McFerrin. It was number 1 on the Billboard Hot 100 chart for two weeks in September 1988 and won Best Song of the Year prize at the 1989 Grammy Awards.

Match the words and phrases on the left to the definitions on the right.

philosopher	a deep thinker; someone makes theories about life
pursuit of happiness	a truth; something that usually happens
liberty	approve; agree to; declare
human rights	freedom
possessions	good; effective; sound; useful
makes sense	imagine; picture in your mind
affirm	natural rights
visualize	the opposite of 'positive'
a fact of life	things that you own
positive	to be logical; reasonable
negative	trying to achieve happiness

Comprehension Check

1. What does 'the goal of humanity' mean?
2. What does 'basic human rights' mean?
3. Where do most people look for happiness?
4. Where can happiness and success be found?
5. What is 'Affirmation'?
6. What is 'Visualization'?
7. How can we become more positive?

Think for Yourself

- [ ] Do you ever affirm or visualize? Do you want to try?
- [ ] How can you be more positive in your life?
- [ ] What do you think 'success' means?
- [ ] What do you think 'happiness' means?
- [ ] If you could choose only two of the things below, which would you choose?

> - [ ] a good job   - [ ] fame   - [ ] family   - [ ] friendship   - [ ] health   - [ ] love   - [ ] money   - [ ] peace
> - [ ] possessions   - [ ] security   - [ ] travel

Background Information

Did you know?

- [ ] The world's happiest countries are 1) Nigeria, 2) Mexico, 3) Venezuela, 4) El Salvador, and 5) Puerto Rico.
- [ ] The world population is, on average, less than 65% happy.
- [ ] People can be trained to be 25% happier through various training programs in from 2 to 10 weeks.
- [ ] The income of Americans has gone up 2.5 times over the last 50 years, but their happiness level has not changed.
- [ ] The happiest people love their family and friends, don't care about possessions, focus 100% even in daily activities and forgive easily.
- [ ] Richard St. John (the writer of *Spike's Guide to Success*) defines happiness and success in 8 words: 1. passion 2. work 3. good 4. focus 5. push 6. serve 7. ideas 8. persist.

Discussion Us Groups

- Talk about the questions below.
- Use the Conversation Strategies at the bottom of the page.

1. Who is the most successful person you know?
   ▶ Tell the others about this person.

2. Who is the happiest person you know?
   ▶ Tell the others about this person.
   ▶ Is he/she the same person as in Question 1?

3. Is it possible to be successful and happy?
   ▶ Why? Why not? Support your opinion.

4. What was the happiest time in your life?
   ▶ Talk about it.

5. What does success mean for you?
   ▶ Tell the others about it.

6. Can money buy happiness?
   ▶ Why? Why not?

7. Does health equal happiness?
   ▶ Explain your opinion.

8. What makes you unhappy?
   ▶ What? Where? When? Why?

9. Are some people born successful?
   ▶ Why do you think that way?

10. What do you need to do to be successful?
    ▶ Explain your opinion.

Conversation Strategies

Why do you think happiness and money don't always go together?

Listing reasons:

For one thing,	And another thing …
The main thing is …	Besides that,
The main reason is …	On top of that,
The most important reason is …	Furthermore,

you can't buy happiness.

happiness is a state of mind.

Dialogue

- Listen to Track 58 on the CD-Rom.
- Read the dialogue with your partner.
- Perform the dialogue together.
- Change roles. Perform the dialogue again.

Key Words and Expressions

lottery
a game of chance, using numbers

gambling
playing a game of chance for money

hooked
addicted; captivated; dependant

"I bet."
"I'm sure you're right." "Right."

The American Dream
the idea that anyone can achieve a comfortable life through hard work, courage and determination

(Mrs. Brown is sitting at a table, choosing lottery numbers.)

Mrs. Brown	Let me see. 32, 55, 27, …
Ji-hye	What are you doing, Mrs. Brown?
Mrs. Brown	Hello, Ji-hye. I'm choosing lottery numbers.
Ji-hye	Isn't that gambling?
Mrs. Brown	I suppose you could call it that. But don't worry, I'm not hooked!
Ji-hye	Do you have any chance of winning anything?
Mrs. Brown	Not really, but you know what they say, 'You've got to be in it to win it.'
Ji-hye	And what if you win?
Mrs. Brown	We'll have a long vacation, for a start.
Ji-hye	I bet. But aren't you happy as you are?
Mrs. Brown	Of course, Ji-hye. I've got a wonderful family. What more could I want?
Ji-hye	So the lottery is just a game?
Mrs. Brown	That's right. You can't buy happiness or success.
Ji-hye	So how can you get them?
Mrs. Brown	That's a good question. I would say passion and hard work.
Ji-hye	I see.
Mrs. Brown	That's the American Dream, after all.

Dialogue Quiz

1. Why is Mrs. Brown choosing numbers?
2. What does Ji-hye think of the lottery?
3. Does Mrs. Brown expect to win anything?
4. Is Mrs. Brown happy?
5. What advice does she give to Ji-hye?
6. What is the American Dream?

Success Interview: Ideas

- If you could interview a successful person (alive or dead), who would it be?
- Would you choose a sportsperson, emperor, king, movie star, singer, writer, or someone else?
- Write the name of your chosen person in the box below.

I would interview …

- Here are some questions you could ask your interviewee.
- Choose five of these and write them on the next page. (Or you can make your own questions.)
- If you are interviewing someone from the past, you need to use the past tense:

"What makes you happy?" "What made you happy?"

How did you become successful?	Who is the most important person in your life?	Does success equal happiness?
What makes you happy?	What makes you unhappy?	What can you do really well?
What can't you do?	What is your favorite color?	Are you optimistic or pessimistic?
What do you like about yourself?	What do you dislike about yourself?	What is your best quality?
What is your worst quality?	What do you do to relax?	What is your biggest worry?
What is your motto?	Do you follow your heart or your brain?	Do you believe in destiny and fate?
Do you believe in life after death?	How important is money?	How important is love?
What do you want to change in yourself?	What do you want to change in other people?	Is there anything you regret?
If you could live your life again, what would you do?	What is your favorite piece of music?	Who is the greatest person you have met?
What is your favorite food?	What is your favorite book?	What do you dream about?
Do you believe in God?	Why did you …?	Why didn't you …?

Success Interview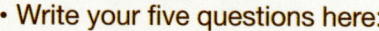

- Write your five questions here:

1 ....
2 ....
3 ....
4 ....
5 ....

- These phrases will help you to present your questions:

Thank you for coming today.	We're very honored.	I'd just like to ask …
I don't want to be personal, but …	I've always wondered ….	I've always wanted to know …
Perhaps you could tell us …	Did you really …?	Do you always …?
When do you …?	Is it true that …?	Can you tell us …?

- These phrases will help you to answer your partner's questions:

Thank you for inviting me.	That's a good question.	I'm glad you asked that.
It's funny you should ask that.	Well, first of all …	I'd just like to say, …
Believe it or not, …	Some people say that …	Off the top of my head, …
Let me think about that.	I can't tell you.	I'd rather not answer.
That's completely false.	That's just a rumor.	Well, to be honest, …

Let's begin the Success Interview!

1. **Student A**: Put your questions to your partner, Student B.
   Student B: Ask who you are playing. Imagine you are that person. Then Answer Student A's questions.
2. Change roles.
   Student B: Put your questions to your partner, Student A.
   Student A: Ask who you are playing. Imagine you are that person. Then Answer Student B's questions.

Speaking Self-assessment

- In Unit 13 (page 112) we looked at your READI skills.
- Let's take another look, now we are almost at the end of the book.
- What are you good at? What do you need to improve?
- Fill in your profile at the bottom of this page.

	1	2	3	4
Range	Not enough range for communication. Poor basic grammar.	Almost enough range for the task. Little control of grammar.	Just enough range for the task. Some control of grammar.	Enough range to communicate easily. Control of grammar.
Ease of Speech	Many hesitations, repetitions, single words and body gestures.	Pauses, single words and short sentences.	Connected speech, short delays. Communication OK despite errors.	No delay. Short sentences. Communication smooth.
Attitude	No enthusiasm. Lack of confidence and motivation. Nervous.	Some desire to perform the task. Lack of confidence and motivation.	Positive attitude. Confidence/ motivation/anxiety do not prevent communication.	Positive attitude, confidence and motivation. Encourages others.
Delivery	Speech slow. No intonation. Pronunciation difficulties.	Low volume, poor intonation, poor stress and word rhythm.	Pronunciation difficulties, but delivery allows communication to continue.	No pronunciation difficulties. Delivery enhances communication.
Interaction	Speaks very little and needs help from the others. No communication strategies.	Tries to communicate. Needs help. Can communicate a little.	Sometimes needs help. Tries to interact. Shows interest in the discussion.	Actively interacts. Good body language. Encourages others.

READI Profile

- How is your profile now?

	1	2	3	4
Range				
Ease of Speech				
Attitude				
Delivery				
Interaction				

There are more reading passages at www.inkbooks.co.kr

18 Learning for Life

Making a Möbius Strip

Task 1

- Get a strip of paper. Write "Front" on one side and "Back" on the other side.

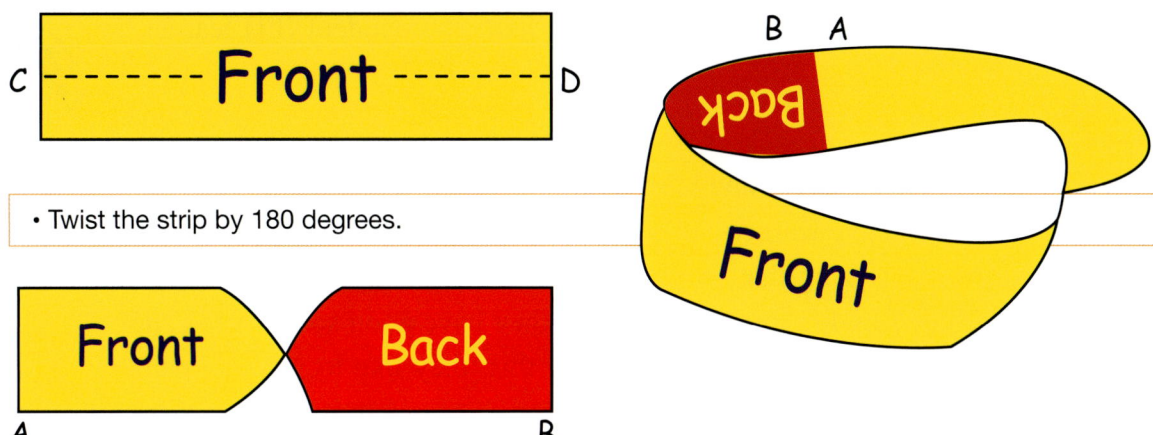

- Twist the strip by 180 degrees.

- Glue the ends (A and B) together. How many sides does your strip have?
- Cut your Möbius Strip in half, from C to D. How many strips do you have now?
- Cut each new strip in half the same way. How many do you have now?

Task 2

- Look at these optical illusions.
- Talk about them together.
- Do you know any more optical illusions?

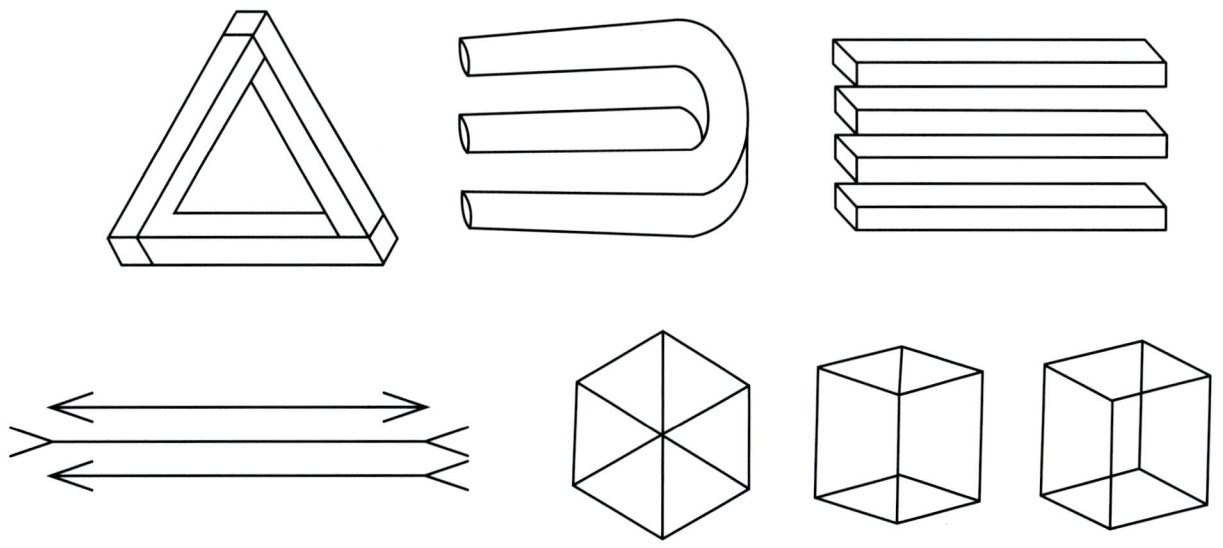

Which is the longest line?   Which way are these boxes facing?

What Do You See?

- Listen to Track 59 on the CD-Rom.
- Read this passage together.
- While you read, match the words and phrases at the bottom of the page.
- Then answer the questions on the next page.

 Groups

Are you a field-dependent (FD) learner, or a field-independent (FI) learner? What do you think?

If you can see only one person in this picture, you are probably field-dependent. FD students often find it difficult to divide something into its parts. They tend to be passive learners, accepting information from the teacher and needing help in analyzing that information. You could say that FD students "can't see the trees for the forest." However, they have good social skills and are good at making relationships. Because of this, they like to work in pairs and groups.

However, if you can see a young woman, an old woman and an old man, you are probably field-independent. FI students are good at analytical thought, so they have little trouble in separating details from the background. If anything, they "can't see the forest for the trees." FI learners don't need the teacher's help when solving problems, and they like to work alone. But they are not so good at making relationships and working with others.

FD and FI people learn in different ways, but these are not the only different learning styles in the classroom. Students can have visual, auditory, tactile and experiential learning styles, in addition to the 9 Multiple Intelligences that everybody has in differing amounts. When you get a chance, try to find out what sort of learner you are. It could help your studies enormously!

Match the words and phrases on the left to the definitions on the right.

probably	consider; break down; evaluate; figure out
divide	connected with the sense of touch
passive	cut; separate
analyze	different types of thinking (logical, musical, etc.)
can't see the trees for the forest	hugely; greatly
can't see the forest for the trees	methods of learning
learning styles	possibly; perhaps; maybe
tactile	quiet; inactive; patient
Multiple Intelligences	This person sees the whole forest first.
enormously	This person sees the trees in the forest first.

There are more reading passages at www.inkbooks.co.kr

Comprehension Check

1. What do 'FD' and 'FI' mean?
2. What does "You can't see the forest for the trees" mean?
3. Describe FD learners.
4. Do FI learners like working in groups?
5. Does everyone have the same Multiple Intelligences?
6. Can you find another word for "learner" in the passage?

Think for Yourself

- ☐ Are you an FD or FI learner?
- ☐ Are the long lines in the picture 1 parallel?
- ☐ Are the central circles in the picture 2 different sizes?
- ☐ Is it possible to be both FD and FI?
- ☐ What type of learner are you?

Picture 1

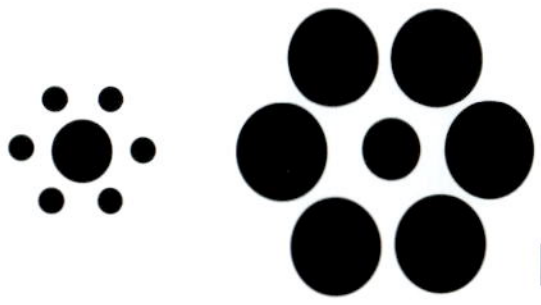

Picture 2

Background Information

Did you know?

- ☐ There are four learning styles:
  - Visual (seeing)
  - Kinesthetic (moving)
  - Auditory (hearing)
  - Tactile (touching)
- ☐ There are 9 Multiple Intelligences:
  - Kinesthetic – good with the body
  - Linguistic – good at languages
  - Intrapersonal – good at helping oneself
  - Musical – good at music
  - Logical – good with numbers
  - Interpersonal – good at relationships
  - Visual/Spatial – good at pictures
  - Naturalistic – good at nature
- ☐ There are 4 types of learners:
  - Innovative learners (who want to improve the world)
  - Analytic learners (who want to improve intellectually)
  - Common sense learners (who want to make things happen)
  - Dynamic learners (who are enthusiastic)

Discussion **Us Groups**

- Talk about the questions below.
- Use the Conversation Strategies at the bottom of the page.

1. **What do you think about optical illusions?**
   ▶ Do they tell us anything about ourselves?
2. **What are your learning styles?**
   ▶ What are your Multiple Intelligences?
3. **How do learning styles affect the way you study?**
   ▶ What is the best way for you to study?
4. **Can we change our learning styles?**
   ▶ Why? Why not? Support your opinion.
5. **Are you good at learning new things?**
   ▶ Explain your thoughts on this topic.
6. **Why are some people better at learning than others?**
   ▶ Support your opinion.
7. **Can learning be fun?**
   ▶ Why? Why not? Explain your opinion.
8. **What tips about learning would you give to other people?**
9. **What good and bad learning experiences have you had?**
10. **Will you stop learning after school?**
    ▶ What do you think of lifelong learning?

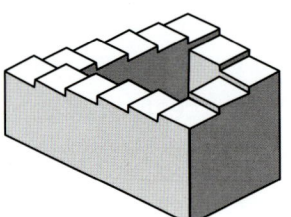

Conversation Strategies

What do you see? What do you think it is?*

Making a guess:
- I'd say …
- I think it's a …
- Perhaps its …
- It looks like …
- I guess it's a …
- It's not easy to say.
- It's hard to say.

Asking other people:
- Any ideas?
- How about you?
- What do you think?
- What would you say?
- What can you see?
- Help me out here.
- Do you mind if I ask you?

*Can you see a woman or a saxophone player, or both?

Dialogue

- Listen to Track 60 on the CD-Rom.
- Read the dialogue with your partners.
- Perform the dialogue together.
- Change roles. Perform the dialogue again.

(Mrs. Brown is sitting on the sofa, looking at Jenny's homework book.)

Grandma Brown	Hello, Helen. What are you looking at?
Mrs. Brown	It's Jenny's homework. It's really interesting. Look at these lines. Are they all straight?
Grandma Brown	It's hard to say. What do you think?
Mrs. Brown	I'm not sure. And how about these circles?
Grandma Brown	The ones in the middle, you mean?
Mrs. Brown	Right. Jenny says here that they are the same size.
Grandma Brown	Hmm. And what are these weird shapes?
Mrs. Brown	Apparently they're personality tests.
Grandma Brown	You're pulling my leg! They're just ink blots.
Mrs. Brown	No, really! We didn't do this sort of homework when I was at school.
Grandma Brown	Neither did we. What's the subject?
Mrs. Brown	Let me see. It's Social Studies.
Grandma Brown	Are you sure? What do these pictures have to do with Social Studies?
Mrs. Brown	It seems they help you find out about your personality.
Grandma Brown	Well, well. We learn something new every day.
Mrs. Brown	I'd better put the book back. Jenny's coming.
Grandma Brown	Right. Turn on the TV. *(Jenny enters the room.)*
Jenny	Hi, mum. Hello Grandma. Have you seen my homework book? I can't find it anywhere.

Key Words and Expressions

weird
unusual or strange

"You're pulling my leg."
"You're not serious." "You're joking."

ink blots
spots of ink on a page

"We learn something new every day."
"I didn't know that."
"That's news to me."

Dialogue Quiz

1. What does Mrs. Brown think about Jenny's homework?
2. Did Helen or her mother do homework like this at school?
3. How do the ink blots help Jenny with Social Studies?
4. What is Jenny looking for? Where do you think it is?
5. What can you find out about ink blot tests?

Trivia game: Ideas

- Did you read the "Background Information" in each Unit (pages 11, 19, 27, … 147)?
- Let's make a Trivia Game based on that information.

Task 1
- Choose 5 items of Background Information from different Units.
- Write them in the boxes.

1.

2.

3.

4.

5.

Task 2
- Change the statements into "Wh" questions or "How" questions.
- For example:

Statement: "Two dogs survived the wreck of the Titanic." (page 19)
Question: "How many dogs survived the wreck of the Titanic?"

1.

2.

3.

4.

5.

Our Questions Us▸Groups

- Talk about your questions with your group members.
- You should have 20 questions altogether.
- Now rank your questions according to their difficulty (100, 50, 20 and 10 points).

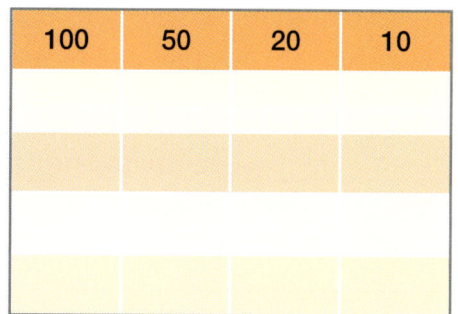

- Write the numbers of your questions in the grid.
- For example, perhaps Q1 is worth 20 points.
- Maybe Q2 is worth 50 points, etc.

Now Let's play the Trivia Game! Us▸Groups

- Choose which group is group A and which is group B.
- Group A: Ask group B for a question for 100, 50, 20 or 10 points.
  [If your answer is correct, write your score in the box below (on the left).]
- Group B: Read the question that group A asked for.
  If group A answers correctly, write their score in the box on the right.
  If group A answers incorrectly, they get no score.
- Group B: Ask group A for a question for 100, 50, 20 or 10 points.
  [If your answer is correct, write your score in the box below (on the left).]
- Group A: Read the question that group B asked for.
  If group B answers correctly, write their score in the box on the right.
  If group B answers incorrectly, they get no score.
- Continue asking questions until all 20 questions have been read out.
- Compare scores between the two groups.

Our scores:

100	50	20	10

Our opponents' scores:

100	50	20	10

Reflect and Review Me

- We have come to the final page.
- It's time to look back on what we have learned.
- It's also time to look forward to what we will do next.

Task
- Fill in this reflection survey.
- Remember, there are no correct answers.
- Just say what you mean and mean what you say!

1	Which was your favorite Unit?	
2	Which was your least favorite Unit?	
3	Which was your favorite reading passage?	
4	Which was your favorite discussion?	
5	Which was your favorite role-play?	
6	Which was your favorite debate?	
7	What did you learn from this book?	
8	What are you better at now?	
9	What do you still need to improve?	
10	What are your future plans for studying?	
11	What are your goals for the future?	
12	How will you achieve those goals?	

Answer Key

Who's Who?
Page 8

Michael's mother is called Grandma Brown. Grandma Brown's son is called Michael. Helen is Michael's wife. Jenny's brother, Kevin, is Seung-min's friend. Jenny is Helen's daughter and Ji-hye's friend. Kim Ji-hye is Jenny's friend, and Kevin's friend is Park Seung-min.

Unit 1
Page 9

Here is the solution to the Favorite Color puzzle:

Most Popular Baby Names in 2015					
USA		UK		Korea	
girls	boys	girls	boys	girls	boys
❶ Olivia	❶ Muhammad	❶ Amelia	❶ Oliver	❶ Seo-yeon	❶ Min-jun
❷ Sophia	❷ Oliver	❷ Olivia	❷ Jack	❷ Seo-yun	❷ Seo-jun
❸ Emily	❸ Jack	❸ Isla	❸ Harry	❸ Ji-u	❸ Ju-won
❹ Amelia	❹ Noah	❹ Emily	❹ Jacob	❹ Seo-hyeon	❹ Ye-jun
❺ Lily	❺ Jacob	❺ Poppy	❺ Charlie	❺ Min-seo	❺ Si-u

Unit 1
Page 16

Time to Think!

1. The fourth child is called Michael.

2.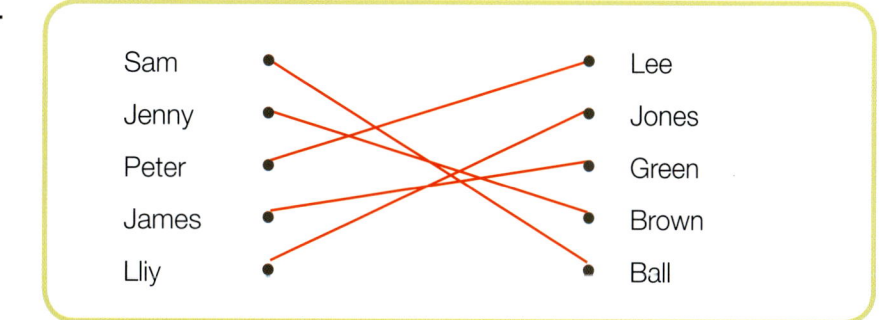

3. I am your sister.

Unit 2
Page 19

RSPCA: Royal Society for the Prevention of Cruelty to Animals
RSPB: Royal Society for the Protection of Birds
WWF: World Wildlife Fund
PAWS: Performing Animals Welfare Society or Philadelphia Animal Welfare Society

Unit 2
Page 24

1. A watchdog.
2. You might step in a poodle (puddle).
3. When you are a mouse.
4. Three blind mice.
5. Because they forgot the words.
6. Because it's too far to walk.

Answer Key

Unit 3
Page 27

I'm as small as an ant, and as big as a whale.
People can hit me, but they can't hurt me.
I dance to the music, though I can't hear.
You can't run away from me. What am I?

Answer: I am your shadow.

Unit 4
Page 32

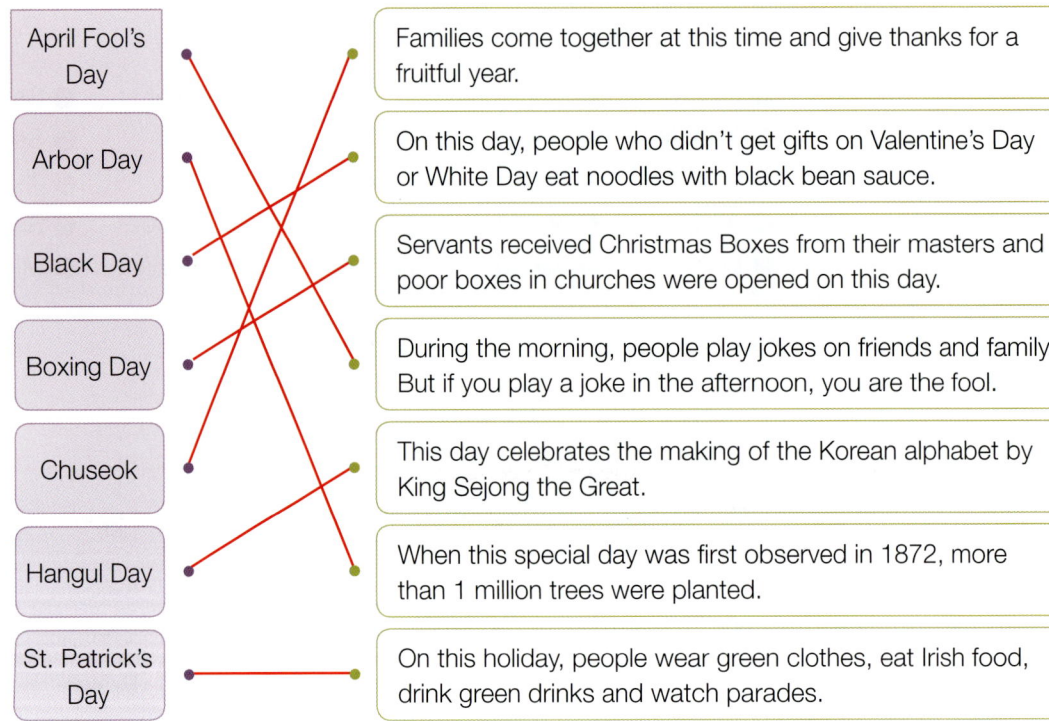

Unit 5
Page 42

The people are: Ban Gi-moon, Kim Yu-na, Park Ji-sung, and Hanna Jang

Unit 5
Page 46

O.W. = Oprah Winfrey (Talk Show Host)
G.W.B. = George W. Bush (President of the USA)
M.T. = Margaret Thatcher (Prime Minister of the UK)
A.L. = Abraham Lincoln (President of the USA)
N.M. = Nelson Mandela (President of South Africa)
M.G. = Mahatma Gandhi

Answer Key

Unit 6
Page 49

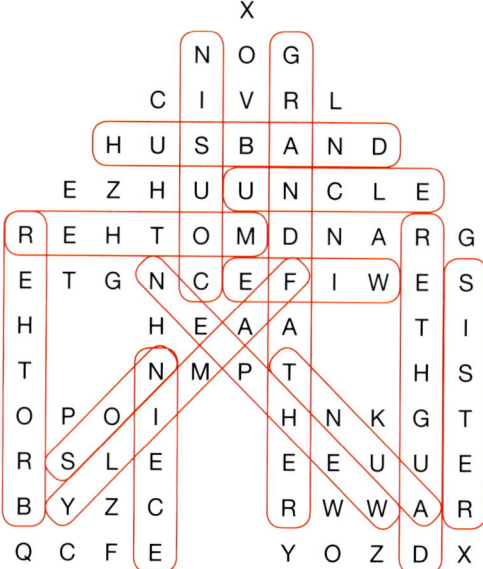

Unit 6
Page 54

1	London is the capital of England.	Fact
2	London is the best city to visit in Europe.	Opinion
3	Spring is the best season to visit London.	Opinion
4	Buckingham Palace is in London.	Fact
5	Arsenal Football Club is in London.	Fact
6	Football is better than baseball.	Opinion
7	Swimming is good for health.	Fact
8	Healthy body, healthy mind.	Opinion
9	Smoking is an unhealthy habit.	Fact
10	Secondhand smoke harms children.	Fact
11	An apple a day keeps the doctor away.	Opinion
12	Family values are important.	Opinion
13	Honesty is the quality of being truthful.	Fact
14	Honesty is the best policy.	Opinion
15	Parents should not punish their children.	Opinion
16	Money can't buy happiness.	Opinion
17	Nature is more important than nurture.	Opinion
18	Like father like son.	Opinion

Answer Key

Unit 11 — Page 89

If your score is 45 to 60, you have a healthy sense of well-being. You are looking after yourself well, and keeping a positive attitude to life.

If your score is 30 to 44, you are making some effort to stay physically and mentally healthy, but you need to work more on this. Be more active. Practice deep breathing every day.

If your score is 15 to 29, you know what you want to do, but you are having difficulty in doing it. Remember that your health is most important. It is not a waste of time to do some exercise three times a week. Pick up a book. Start doing the things you always promised yourself to do.

If your score is below 15, you need to think about your life as soon as possible. What do you want? Are you doing anything to get it? Is money more important than health to you? Do you become angry easily? Do you get stressed easily? Try to get some quiet time to yourself every day. Take a walk and do some deep breathing. Turn the TV off.

Unit 11 — Page 96

1. Turn the page upside down and you will see that the table is number 87.
2. You should light the match first, or you won't be able to light anything else.
3. The two men play chess with different people. For example, if the men were called A and B, then A played with C and B played with D.

Unit 12 — Page 97

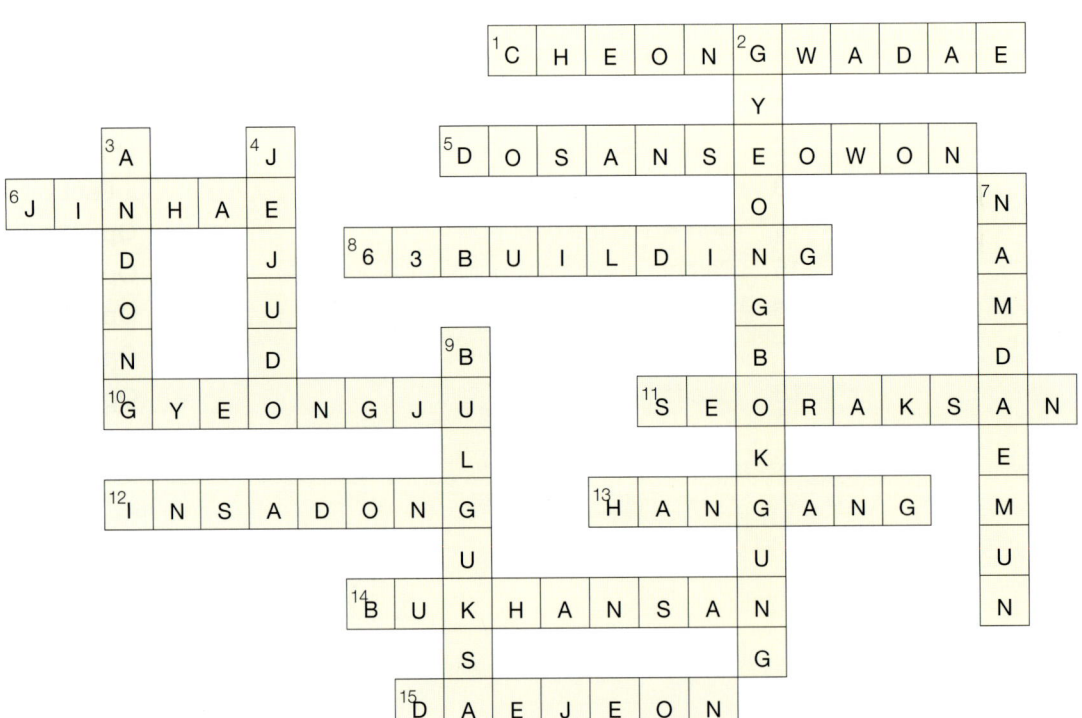

Answer Key

Unit 13 Page 105

3. He told her never to open it, and gave the key to her husband.
4. Pandora was very curious about the box.
6. One day he fell asleep, and she stole the key.
8. Pandora tried to catch them, but it was too late.
9. Pandora sat and cried. Then the last thing flew out.
10. The last thing was hope.
1. Pandora was a beautiful woman.
5. She asked her husband to open it, but he always said "No."
7. She opened the box and all the troubles of the world flew out.
2. The King of the Gods gave her a little box.

Unit 13 Page 106

1 Koreans; 2 Australian Aborigines; 3 American Indians; 4 Ethiopians

Unit 13 Page 109

Giparang's lover is called Seonwha.

Unit 15 Page 128

This problem was solved in 1736 by Leonhard Euler. His proof led to graph theory and topology. His solution? In fact he showed that it can't be done!

Unit 16 Page 136

The 9th person is playing chess. This is usually an activity that needs two people.